Risk and ageing

Hazards and Helping

Series editor: C. Paul Brearley

Forthcoming books in the series:

Risk and Children
Social Work and Psychiatric Emergencies

RISK AND AGEING

C. Paul Brearley

With M.R.P. Hall, P.M. Jefferys,
R. Jennings and S. Pritchard

ROUTLEDGE & KEGAN PAUL
London, Boston, Melbourne and Henley

First published in 1982
by Routledge & Kegan Paul Ltd
39 Store Street, London WC1E 7DD,
9 Park Street, Boston, Mass. 02108, USA,
296 Beaconsfield Parade, Middle Park,
Melbourne, 3206, Australia and
Broadway House, Newtown Road,
Henley-on-Thames, Oxon RG9 1EN
Printed in Great Britain by
Redwood Burn Ltd, Trowbridge, Wiltshire
Contributions by M.R.P. Hall, P.K. Jefferys,
R. Jennings and S. Pritchard © Routledge
& Kegan Paul 1982
All other contributions and editorial matter
© C. Paul Brearley 1982

ISBN 0 7100 9080 3

CONTENTS

ACKNOWLEDGMENTS

My thanks are due to many people for their contribution to the ideas in this book. I am particularly grateful to Jane Mountain for her permission to use some of the case material which is included.

NOTES ON CONTRIBUTORS

C. Paul Brearley, Senior Lecturer in Social Work, University College of North Wales, Bangor.

Michael Hall, Professor of Geriatric Medicine, University of Southampton.

Peter Jefferys, Consultant Psychiatrist, Northwick Park and Shenley Hospitals, and Clinical Research Centre, Harrow.

Rosemary Jennings, Senior Social Worker, Northwick Park and Shenley Hospitals, Harrow.

Stewart Pritchard, Principal Officer, Fieldwork, Social Services Department, Gwynedd County Council.

INTRODUCTION

Attitudes towards older people involve a mixture of sometimes
contradictory and often uncomfortable perceptions and misper-
ceptions. As long ago as 1947 the Rowntree Report on the problems of ageing concluded:

> In recent years there has been a considerable awakening of
> public interest in the problems of old age, an awakening that
> has manifested itself in a sympathetic attitude to old people and
> in a widespread desire to be generous to them. The Committee
> are in full sympathy with this attitude but they have felt bound
> to take into account another point of view, based not on any
> lack of sympathy with the aged but on a recognition of the
> country's strictly limited resources of wealth and labour, and
> the rapidly growing proportion of old people in the total pop-
> ulation (p. 95).

Many people would probably find this a reasonable statement of
the position in Britain thirty-five years later. There is still an
evident concern and a general willingness to make provision for
the older population (Townsend, 1980), but although many seem
to assume that great strides have been made since the late 1940s
there remain many inconsistencies, inequalities and inadequacies
in our social provision for older people (Bosanquet, 1978). A
major feature of the present situation arises from changes in the
proportion of very old people in the population. David Hobman,
director of Age Concern England makes the point very clearly:

> The possibility of one-fifth of the total population in retire-
> ment from active employment would have been unthinkable at
> the beginning of the twentieth century and even recent social
> planning has made no adequate provisions for a society in which
> one in every twenty-five people will be over seventy-five, and
> one in every hundred over eighty-five in less than a decade
> (1978, p. 13).

In this book the detailed implications of ageing in terms of its
costs and some of its gains both for society and for individuals
will be explored. It is clear that social and health-service provisions for older people are becoming more and more provisions
for the very old. It is common to hear discussions of 'the problem
elderly' or of old people 'at risk' or 'in need'. One important contribution of this book will be to explore some of the meanings of

the words that are used - need, risk, safety, protection - in relation to older people. A brief description of the situation of one older person will illustrate some of the issues. The following description was written by a social worker after her first visit to Mr C one day early in January, following a request from a GP for help in persuading him to go into hospital and for arrangements for the cat to be fed.

Mr C was living in an extremely large, privately rented, three-storey terraced house which was in such a state of disrepair that from the outside it appeared derelict. Burst pipes had flooded his bedroom, bathroom and toilet and he was currently eating, sleeping and living in one exceedingly damp and draughty room on the ground floor. The only source of heat in the whole house was a coal-fire in this room. One large window had recently been broken by local youths and rather unsuccessfully boarded up subsequently by Mr C.

In the centre of the room was a rickety old step ladder over which were draped loops of electric cable running from the dim electric light bulb to the television. Sanitary arrangements were appalling. The bath and toilet were blocked and, apart from the burst pipes, whenever it rained water dripped through missing slates on the roof. The bathroom was on the first floor up a steep flight of stairs which Mr C had not been able to climb for the past 3 weeks, due to his chest problems. During this time he had been using the old kitchen sink with one cold water tap and a bucket for all his needs.

Mr C's appearance was extremely dirty; he was unshaven and generally unkempt - not surprisingly given the lack of washing facilities. He was physically a tiny, bent man looking much older than his 68 years. He opened the door wearing pyjamas and a very dirty dressing gown and immediately apologised for his appearance and the state of the house. The exertion of answering the door left him breathless for some minutes, however, he seemed quite happy for me to enter the house and speak to him.

Questioning revealed that he had lived in the house for twenty years. He was an only child and initially had lived there with his parents and an uncle and aunt. When he married, his wife also moved in. Twelve years before his parents had moved to a pensioners' flat. As his uncle and aunt had by then died Mr C took on the house tenancy. This he had been most unwilling to do since even at that time the house was in poor condition and the landlord was refusing to carry out repairs. Mr C believed, however, that his parents would only be allowed to move if he remained in the house and he made sure he was on the council housing waiting list.

Soon after his parents moved his wife left him and a few months later a girl-friend moved in. Shortly after this his father died and his mother became ill and had both legs amputated: she died six months later. Mr C made all the funeral arrangements, at the same time nursing his girl-friend who was seriously ill with cancer. The strain was such that he suffered a severe coronary and after two months was discharged from hospital unable to walk more than 500 yards. His girlfriend had died so he was on his own and also unable to get a job as he had previously held unskilled manual jobs.

The impact of the succession of personal tragedies had resulted in a prolonged period of depression, self-neglect and drinking. Mr C's only surviving relatives were his wife from whom he had never been legally separated but whose address he no longer knew, and two cousins whom he had not seen for over ten years. He had no contact with neighbours and, although he claimed to have friends at the pub, none ever came to the house.

Clearly Mr C is existing in extremely difficult circumstances both in his own terms and those of the caring professionals who encountered him. These difficulties can be seen in a number of ways. A predominant feature of the description is the accumulation of losses that he has experienced - loss of family, friends, health, employment, adequate accommodation, to name but a few. One consequence is that he could be described as being in need of substitutes, including health-care facilities, good housing, friendly support and practical help.

But there is another dimension: he is leading not only a deprived existence but he is also living in conditions of uncertainty. He is exposed to a large number of practical hazards - damp, lack of adequate sanitation, faulty electric wiring, steep stairs, breathlessness - which all help to create a situation in which something might go wrong. He is also exposed to a number of less tangible pressures - his lack of neighbours or other supporters, his reluctance to go into hospital (later said to be related to his mother's experience in the same hospital), his self-neglect, and so on. All of these factors combine to create the possibility of some dangerous outcome occurring. In this sense he is very much 'at risk'.

THE NATURE OF RISK

For a full exploration of the approach used in this book the reader is recommended to read the introductory book in this series, 'Risk in Social Work' (Brearley, 1982). The main argument will be briefly summarized here.

There are two broad elements to understanding risk. The first of these is the estimation or measurement of risk and the second is the evaluation of the risk. Risk estimation includes two dimensions. One factor involves an estimation of the probability that an outcome will occur: this includes such concepts as possibility and likelihood. The second dimension involves the recognition that in any one situation a number of possible outcomes may occur, each of which has a relative probability: this can be referred to as the variation in possible outcomes. Risk, in this sense, is a relative term based on probability and the theme which most authors in the field of risk theory seem to accept is that which relates risk with potential variation in loss outcomes and which emphasizes the variation of actual from probable loss.

There is a difference between the objective variation in possible outcomes and the subjective response to being in an uncertain situation. Objective probability is the proportion of times a particular outcome would occur in the long run assuming that underlying conditions remain unchanged. Subjective probability refers to estimates of the objective probability which will vary among people facing the same objective probability.

There are, then, two key questions in estimating risk:

1 What are the possible outcomes accessible in the state of current knowledge?
2 What is the probability that each of the possible outcomes will occur?

Risk evaluation involves attaching a value to each of the known outcomes and a process of balancing the relative value or utility of each outcome in reaching a decision. Some reference will be made later to practical issues involved in arriving at safety judgments about older people. The judgment of safety involves measuring the risk and deciding about the acceptability and inevitability of risk. Pragmatically, safety is a term which will be used to describe a situation in which risks are acceptable.

A number of basic definitions can be taken from this discussion which is drawn primarily from writings in the field of risk and insurance:

1 Risk refers to the relative variation in possible loss outcomes.
2 Probability refers to the relative likelihood of outcomes.
3 Uncertainty refers to the subjective responses of the person who is exposed to risk.

A second set of definitions can be drawn from considerations of scientific and technological risk. Here the concern is not so much with the range and variation in possible costs as with the probability relationships between events or situations and their outcomes. In order to protect against loss actually occurring it is necessary to clarify the likelihood of that loss and the factors that may bring it about. Two further definitions are therefore added.

4 Hazard refers to any factor - an action, event, lack or deficiency, or other entity - which introduces the possibility or increases the probability of an undesirable outcome.
5 Danger refers to a feared outcome of a hazard which is either expected to be a loss outcome or is associated with loss in the expectation of the observer.

In the case of Mr C, for example, the steep stairs are a hazard to the danger of falling, his poor health is a hazard to the danger of becoming socially isolated, and the isolation is a hazard to loneliness and self-neglect. The importance of the hazard-danger distinction is that it makes it possible to distinguish between the likelihood of a feared outcome and its importance or value to the individual. Only if the things that are feared are identified and given a relative value is it possible to begin ordering priorities. Action is therefore related to what is felt to be most important in relation to the relative likelihood of outcomes. On an oversimplified level this may involve decisions about whether the danger to Mr C's health is of more importance than the danger to his right to choose for himself how to live or die.

The use of the terms hazard and danger also gives a basis for a framework within which to analyse the over-all risk. In the following simplified example the concept of hazard has been divided into predisposing (or predictive) hazards (those which make danger possible) and situational hazards (those which make danger very probable): this is a distinction on the basis of the degree of probability. Strengths in the situation have also been included since a full risk analysis includes a balancing of hazards and strengths which may offset the effects of hazards. The list is illustrative not comprehensive.

	Predisposing hazards	Situational hazards	Strengths	Dangers
Mr C	Age. Poor health. Isolation. Lack of social contacts, etc.	Burst pipes. Faulty wiring. Deteriorating physical condition. Poor heating, etc.	Social Worker. GP. Willingness to discuss problems.	Further deterioration of health. Depression/suicide. Cold/hypothermia. Loss of right to self-determination. Self-neglect.

This framework provides an aid to clearer decision making and can be extended to others involved in the situation. A danger to the social worker, for example, is that he may both feel responsible and be held responsible if he does not take action to encourage or persuade Mr C to go into hospital.

These issues have been explored fully elsewhere and space does not permit further development at this point. Throughout this book it will be assumed that action and decisions will be concerned not only with current needs (seen as relative deficiencies, lacks or losses), but also with the implications of need for the future. Decisions about care for older people are made on the basis of perceived need but also on the basis of anticipated and predicted dangers. Need and risk are inextricably bound up together but the assumption here is that it is appropriate in working with older people to stress future possibilities as much as to meet existing need. It should therefore be added that risk taking is an inevitable and often a desirable part of action with older people. 'At riskness' is the passive component of risk in which the actor is exposed to the possibility of loss and damage. Risk taking involves a conscious decision to put something at stake; to accept exposure to possible loss in the hope of relative gain (or reduced loss).

To achieve the basic objective of exploring issues in risk analysis and management in relation to older people this book is presented broadly in two parts. In the first part, general ideas about the nature of ageing and knowledge about the situation of older people are presented. Chapter 1 outlines some of the most commonly discussed theoretical approaches in the field of gerontology and considers these in relation both to an over-all view and to the experience of individual older people. Chapter 2 identifies the more common hazards to older people as a group and discusses why some older people are more likely than others to be exposed to serious danger. The final three chapters have a more immediate focus on practical provision through a discussion of social work, of mental health and mental disorder, and of health care. Chapter 3 provides a link between what might be regarded as the theoretical or academic knowledge presented in the earlier chapters and the more pragmatic practice knowledge of the second half of the book through a consideration of assessment, decision making and the use of practical resources.

If we are to make appropriate provision for older people, it seems essential that policy and practice should be informed by the growing body of theory and research as well as by the pragmatic day-to-day experience of practitioners. This book sets out to bring these perspectives together in relation to the general theme of risk analysis and management. The emphasis will be on practical hazards and their management but this must be seen within a more general context of risk, recognizing the importance of positive as well as negative outcomes in uncertain situations. Risk management is not only about caution and protection but is also about gambling and hope of future gain. Working with older people does not have to be based on negative assumptions – informed optimism plays a part in effective risk taking.

GENERAL NOTES

1 Where the gender of an older person, worker or other person is not defined by the circumstances described, he or she has been referred to throughout in the masculine gender. Since the majority of older people are women such references should obviously not be taken to imply male or female. The use of the masculine gender has been adopted for convenience.

2 It has often been argued that the terms 'elderly' or 'old

people', 'the aged', etc. confirm those who are over a certain age in a position which creates an inappropriate impression of difference based solely on age criteria. To avoid this I have tried to use the term 'older people' throughout, except where quoting directly from others. Sometimes this leads inevitably to a rather clumsy use of words but on balance I believe this to be preferable to furthering a separation which is based only on age.

1 THE STUDY OF AGE AND AGEING

Some initial issues arise which have a bearing on our ability to proceed to a discussion of knowledge and prediction in work with older people. The outline that follows of explanations, models and propositions in the field of social gerontology is intended to throw some light on both the experience of ageing and of being older; it is an attempt to present ways of understanding age and ageing. These ideas must be seen in the context of a number of reservations; what we 'know' about the subject is still very much bound up with what we believe about it both in the sense that many of our ideas derive from untested assumptions and also in the sense that some writers entangle their beliefs about what is with what should be. Many of the ideas draw from the North American context and are untested in Britain. Much of our knowledge about Britain's older people relates to quantitative data and relatively little work has been done on the development of theory for use in explaining or predicting events. It should also be borne in mind that some kinds of knowledge of old age can only be possessed by those who are experiencing it.

The variety and extent of knowledge and ideas is considerable and a summary or review is difficult but some attempt to describe ways of understanding ageing and the position of older people is necessary before proceeding to consider action and risk. Understanding, however, is a word that is used to express an attitude or orientation as much as any actual knowledge or competency. This chapter is partly explanatory but also includes an element of advocacy; the approach presented is intended to encourage optimism.

UNDERSTANDING AGEING : THEORETICAL PERSPECTIVES

It seems to be important to begin with a consideration of attitudes. There are two central reasons for this: first, gerontological writers have given a lot of attention to myths and stereotypes; and, second, attitudes are said to play an important part in the development (or lack of development) of practical health and social services for older people. One of the most influential writers in the field has been Robert Butler who coined the word 'ageism' to refer to a 'process of systematic stereotyping of, and discrimination against people because they are old, just as racism and sexism accomplish this with skin colours and gender' (1975, p. 12). According to Butler, ageism involves a wide range of phenomena including stereotypes and myths, outright disdain and dislike or simply the avoidance of contact. Many other authors have developed the theme of myths about ageing and it would not be difficult to provide a substantial list. Among the most commonly cited are the so-called 'tranquillity myth' and the 'inevitability myth'. The former refers to the assumption that old age is a time of relative peace when people can relax and enjoy the fruits of their lifetime's labour (Saul, 1974); old age is positively portrayed but, as Butler puts it 'as a kind of adult fairyland'. The inevitability myth, on the other hand, presents an overdrawn picture of a more negative kind. It implies the preconceptions, for instance, 'that all older people are similar, that ageing involves various irreversible illnesses (mental or physical), a "fixed" state of mind, and shrinking capacities, and that an aged person is ipso facto, rigid, unchangeable, sterile and dependent' (Saul, 1974, p. 21).

It is important to be aware of the existence and potential influence of stereotypes, but at least one writer has recognized that the preoccupation with ageism creates its own potential problems. Kalish (1979) argues that what he calls 'New Agism' is as much found in advocates of older people as among their antagonists. New Agism has a number of characteristics. Briefly, it stereotypes 'the elderly' as the least capable, least healthy and least alert of those who are older; it sees the older person as relatively helpless and in need of services; it encourages the development of services without considering the possible impact of those services on people's power to control their own lives; and it emphasizes the unpleasant existence faced by the elderly by criticizing society in general. The more evangelical gerontology becomes in advocating on behalf of 'the elderly' the more it confirms their powerless and rejected status. Although the argument has more than a ring of truth, as a position of 'radical pessimism', it offers little in the way of progress. Kalish is himself led to a familiar position in advocating a Personal Growth model:

> The later years can be a period of optimum personal growth. Not for everyone: some are not in adequate health, some are too financially restricted, some have been socialized in their early years in ways of thinking and behaving that make later growth impossible. But the later years can be a time for growth (1979, p. 40).

There are disadvantages in stressing the negative elements in attitudes to the elderly but they can hardly be denied.

Several factors are likely to influence the attitudes of professionals to work with older people:

1 'Failure models' of old age which assume reduced hope of change.
2 Associated with this, the low status of older people is often

reflected in low status for those who work with them.
3 Linked also to this is the relative underdevelopment of
training for work in this field in Britain. There are, of
course, some notable exceptions in the development of geriatrics in some medical schools during the 1970s and the
growth of nurse training in specialist aspects of the work.
In the field of social work, however, training for work with
older clients remains very underdeveloped.
4 Social and health service resources for older people are expensive and have developed substantially in the last 20
years but they remain inadequate for the tasks to be done.
There is often, therefore, depressingly little that can realistically be done to help some older people in need.
5 It has also been suggested that, since older people are more
likely to die, work with this group is both a constant re-
minder of one's own mortality, and frequently involves the
distress and grief of loss. It is hard to see the death of a
patient or client as success.
6 Finally, the ambivalence remains. When older people compete
with, for example, children for scarce resources their need
for care may be obvious but the argument that they have
had their turn and should make way for others persists.

Returning to an earlier comment, it is not the intention of this
book to foster or emphasize a pessimistic view of old age. A realistic appraisal of what is possible, through careful analysis, a
deeper understanding, and a creative use of resources is likely
to lead to a clearer view of what can be achieved.

Successful and unsuccessful ageing
An important aspect of the core of gerontology has been the
stress on normal ageing, on what is usual. The attempts to describe and understand what is normal, however, do not necessarily link easily to what might be regarded as successful ageing
either in the view of the ageing person or in the view of a wider
society. It is neither necessary to be like everyone else to be
satisfied, nor necessary to begin a review of theoretical approaches to ageing with the assumption that older people are a hom-
ogeneous group. It is possible to consider descriptions of what
happens to a majority of people as they get older in a particular
social context, but it will not be assumed here either that all
older people are the same or that they should all approximate to
a standard.
   Ageing is a process through time and it is therefore appropriate to begin with the developmental view. The life course, or
what has sometimes been called the life path, is seen as an
ordered progression of changes through life from birth to old
age and death. Considerations of the life course have taken a
number of forms. One approach stresses the ways in which social
age influences and regulates the way an individual sees himself
and how he behaves: 'Individuals develop a mental map of the life

cycle; they anticipate that certain events will occur at certain times; and they internalize a social clock that tells them whether they are on or off time' (Neugarten and Hagestad, 1976, p. 35). Central themes of the developmental perspective have commonly drawn from developmental psychology and stress three assumptions: that people continue to grow and change through life; that adulthood can be seen as a sequential, orderly progression, and that development during adulthood is a continuous process but that it is significantly different from development during childhood (Kimmell, 1974). The approach has considerable advantages since it provides a basis for over-all consideration of issues whilst enabling consideration of significant 'life tasks' during the process. However, as Bromley has pointed out, there are complications since, although growth to adolescence may be relatively orderly and well regulated, adult ageing 'can be described as an increasingly disorderly and undirected process of biological and behavioural disorganization and desperation' (1974, p. 29).

An associated view of personality development emphasizes the importance of 'life tasks'. Erikson (1964), for instance, proposes that there are eight stages of integration to be achieved in the development of the ego. These range from an initial stage of trust versus mistrust to a final stage of ego-integrity versus despair. Primarily this final stage is said to involve an acceptance of an order and meaning in the totality of an individual's life - past, present and future. From the safety of this integrated view of the totality of life the inevitability of death can be viewed with acceptance rather than fear. A developmental model therefore offers both an over-all perspective on common life-course events and life tasks, and a basis for considering the individual's experience of his personal development. In this latter sense the concept of adaptation is often introduced both as a personality dimension ('this person is well-adjusted', etc.) and as a behavioural description ('this person has made adjustments or adaptations to accommodate to certain circumstances'). Although a number of studies have attempted to characterize and classify successfully and unsuccessfully adapted people, there are substantial difficulties, since satisfaction and adaptation have to be seen within their social context as well as in relation to the subjective experience of the individual.

Turning next to sociological approaches to the study of ageing, Townsend (1976) has identified two groups of thinking. One group of writers have stressed adjustment to and detachment from social roles, while a second see the elderly as direct or indirect victims of a divisive and unequal industrial society.

The importance of social roles has played a central part in much of the development of the sociology of ageing. Probably the most influential, if one of the most depressing examples, is the disengagement approach which has been widely debated and researched. Originally proposed by Cumming and Henry (1961), disengagement theory suggests that the social process of ageing includes a reduction of involvement in social roles for the individual which is paralleled by a reduced need for such involvement. Disengagement is a triple withdrawal; the loss of roles, a contraction in contacts, and a decline in the commitment to norms and values. The suggestion, then, is that as people grow older society demands less from them and they do not necessarily find this dissatisfying. In its original form the theory might be - and sometimes has been - taken to mean that all old people want to be left in peace and quiet to enjoy a gradual withdrawal from involvement. Clearly, in the light of the discussion that has gone before, this kind of generalization is too sweeping and disengagement theory is now rarely defended in its original terms (Maddox, 1973). There is little evidence, for example, that the number or intensity of social contacts decreases independently of ill health and infirmity or poverty, neither is there evidence of declining commitment to norms or values except perhaps in extreme age or with the onset of mental frailty (Townsend, 1976). More recently disengagement theorists have emphasized that involvement with others is not an essential requirement of satisfaction or adjustment in old age. It is possible, in other words, to be uninvolved with others or segregated from role activity and still be satisfied.

The concept of successful ageing has sometimes been equated with life satisfaction and morale (Havighurst, 1961) and sometimes with survival and with good health (Palmore, 1979). Palmore argues that 'a more comprehensive definition of successful ageing would combine all three of these elements: survival (longevity), health (lack of disability), and life satisfaction (happiness)' (1979, p. 427). This position links closely with what has become known as the activity theory of ageing and which has often been contrasted with the disengagement approach. Broadly the activity theory proposes that there is a close association between an individual's level of social activity and participation and his feeling of well-being or life satisfaction (Lemon et al., 1972). In a small study in the south of England, Knapp (1977) found that the level of life satisfaction felt by older people in his sample was positively related to the level of activity. However, he warns against generalization from the limited findings and highlights the potential influence of personality, in particular, on whether or not people experience high or low levels of activity positively or negatively. It is also worth mentioning that Knapp warns against the assumption that the disengagement and activity approaches are directly comparable and that verification of one represents refutation of the other. They are not directly comparable and do deal with different phenomena. Some other support for the activity theory assumptions has been produced. Palmore (1979), for instance, concludes from a longitudinal survey that two of the strongest explanatory factors in predicting successful ageing are physical activity and secondary group activity. This was true for both men and women, and for men work satisfaction was also important. Successful ageing in this study was defined as survival to the age of 75, a lack of disability, and high scores on ratings of contentment.

A rather different approach is that of Rose (in Rose and Peterson, 1965) who argues that because older people have many problems in common, such as low income, disability and poor mobility, it is possible to talk of a sub-culture of ageing. Rose suggests that there is a positive affinity among older people which, like the rejection of older people by younger groups, is based partly on their physical limitations (and interest, therefore, in a calm, physically undemanding existence), partly on their common generation experiences, and partly on the low value placed on inefficiency or non-productivity. The result of these common pressures or attractions, Rose suggests, is that older people tend to develop shared beliefs and identity. Rose predicted, then, that concentrated interaction among older people would lead to participation in an aged sub-culture, the development of ageing and group consciousness and enhanced self-conceptions. This view had a less central role in discussion than disengagement and activity theories but has some modified support in recent studies (Longino et al., 1980).

Writing from an interactionist perspective Rosow (1974) argues that old people in industrialized society have little power, and are consequently devalued and devalue themselves. Older people, he suggests, are viewed in insidious stereotypes, are excluded from social opportunities, lose roles and confront severe role ambiguity in later life. Another, not dissimilar, view describes the problems of ageing as problems of decreasing power resources (Dowd, 1975). Older people are said to be increasingly weak in terms of the balance of social exchange, in relation to those they interact with; the imbalance in the exchange ratio compels the older person to exchange compliance to the wishes or demands of younger people for continued support and sustenance. In a development of this approach Dowd (1980) conceptualizes social exchange between younger and older age groups as a 'boundary crossing' in which the older partner must learn the decision rules appropriate to interaction in a younger stratum. The older partner in the exchange is in a double bind: access to power resources declines with age placing the person in a position of negotiating from weakness and at the same time resources are exchanged for less than they would be if held by a younger person.

One further addition to the consideration of social roles may be useful. Most discussions of roles and ageing emphasize role loss. Blau (1973) argues that it is more useful to conceive of some changes associated with old age as role exits and emphasizes that they may signal entry to a roleless status rather than the acquisition of new roles. Role exit is proposed as a more neutral term than role loss and Blau identifies three kinds of effects on individuals. It produces changes in 'associational life', in self-concept and in mood.

The disadvantage of these theories or approaches seems to rest particularly on their generality. They often assume a passive or compliant position of the elderly and a commonality amongst them as a group and the evidence that the elderly can be viewed in such broad, homogenous terms is sparse. A more recent approach has attempted to relate the common experiences of older people, which exist by virtue of them having lived through a similar time span in the same cultural environment, to the obvious fact that growing old is different for each individual. Johnson (1976) has described life as a biographical career, emphasizing the uniqueness of the human biography rather than the commonality of experience. In his terms, what social gerontologists have called the process of ageing must be seen as 'a complex of strands running for different lengths of time throughout a life biography and moulding its individuality.' This approach can be linked to a number of works. Rhona and Robert Rapoport (1975), for example, have used a series of biographical case studies to illustrate phases in the life cycle, focusing particularly on retirement and leisure. Abrams (1978) has also illustrated his study of the over 75's with a brief, introductory group biography.

Several writers, then, have recognized the dichotomy in the study of ageing between the concept of old age, referring in general terms to a group of people over a certain age whose interests, experiences and needs have been described as being held in common, and the needs, beliefs and attitudes of individuals within that group. One bridge between these two perspectives is the biographical approach which has close links to developmental approaches in social psychology. The understanding of ageing as a process of change through time for the individual is particularly important for practical helping. Ageing is a process or, for the individual, a collection of intellectual, physical, emotional and social processes involving change and adjustment. There is a difference between ageing as a process which involves everyone to a more or less advanced degree and old age as a social concept, and as a time of life when some people will experience problems, just as some people experience problems at any age, and may therefore need professional help.

As well as being a social process ageing is a biological and physical process. Ageing is associated with some decline in organ and tissue function but most of the symptoms and disabilities afflicting old people result from disease. There is a tendency among laymen, and sometimes among professionals, to assume that failing health and abilities are inevitable and irreversible consequences of ageing (Hall et al., 1978). The effects of ageing are, however, separate from the effects of disease and it is important that this distinction should be made. The changes commonly experienced by ageing people are familiar - greying hair, wrinkling of the skin, changes in fat distribution and particularly sensory changes. Changes in hearing and sight are of particular importance because they contribute to difficulties of communication with the old person.

Intellectual changes with ageing are complex and much of the

evidence provides a basis for little more than generalizations.
There seems to be a tendency for the older person to be slower,
and less adaptable but he has a store of experience and learning to compensate for any losses. The longer he has lived, for
instance, the less likely it is that he will encounter new problems and so any change in problem-solving capacity may be
irrelevant. It may also be that older people are more cautious
(although this may depend on the nature of the gain, or payoff)
(Okun and Elias, 1977) and take longer to make decisions, and
there are also changes in memory capacity (Chown, 1972). It
seems likely that performance in many of the tests used is affected by interest, motivation and educational background and it is
therefore difficult to disentangle age effects from other causes.

One further consideration should be mentioned. It has been
argued earlier that there is an important relationship between
satisfaction and social activity. Another dimension to this debate
comes from physiological research, which seems to suggest a relationship between continuing social and physical activity and life
satisfaction. This argument proposes that

> it is obviously impossible to stop or reverse the passage of
> time, but it is possible to adjust our attitudes and our mode
> of life in such a way that we help ourselves to stay fit and
> lively-minded throughout our life (Gore, 1976, p. 16).

There is certainly an increasing amount of evidence that exercise and stimulation are important components of continuing
activity in later life. If there is a physical reserve capacity which
can be drawn upon by exercise then it is only a short step to the
contention that the typical role performance of the older person
includes an element of reserve capacity to be developed through
social stimulation (Brearley, 1976). Perhaps this view is best
summarized by an exhortation from a remarkable 80-year-old
lady, Eira Davies: 'Medical science is adding years to life and it
is up to the whole community to ensure that life (and not just
existence) is added to those extra years so *Let's get moving*'
(1975, p. 79).

To move towards a more holistic conception of ageing it is necessary to take account of two considerations. First, explanations
must draw broadly from a range of disciplines and, second, there
is a difference between the individual's experience of ageing and
old age and a collective view of older people in general. A full
understanding of the individual can only be grasped within the
social context in which he or she grows old. Some detailed and
valuable approaches to understanding the congruence between
the individual and his environment are available and can be recommended for further study (see, for example, Lawton, 1980;
Kahana, 1980).

A broad view of older people as victims of society sees them as
a direct burden within the capitalist state, since after retirement
they make no direct contribution to either capital or the mode of

production (Corrigan and Leonard, 1978). In these terms the problems of old age exist in a context of material deprivation and solutions are seen not in individual terms but in relation to collective action and increased awareness.

Although approached from a very different standpoint, this can be linked to the debate about how far older people are or should be segregated or integrated into society. On a practical level there is ample evidence that the majority of older people are integrated into their local communities by the services they provide for others and receive in return (Shanas et al., 1968). Equally, however, there is evidence that a substantial minority of older people are isolated from family and other social networks (Abrams, 1980). It has been claimed that social integration is an essential factor in maintaining life satisfaction but there is some evidence that objective social integration has only an indirect impact on morale and that a subjective sense of integration is an important intervening variable (Liang et al., 1980). In other words it is what people feel or believe is important to them which influences their view of themselves in relation to the world. The importance of subjective perception will be explored later.

This theme of the relationship between self perception and the perception of others has been developed within social psychology. An important approach has been put forward by Bengston (1973) who distinguishes the Social Breakdown Syndrome from the Social Reconstruction Syndrome. The former suggests that an individual's sense of self relates to the labels and orientations that society attaches: role loss, vague information about what is appropriate behaviour and lack of reference groups lead to an acceptance of inappropriate role-behaviour. One proposition, for instance, is that some older people are attracted by the relatively clearly defined limits of the sick role and behave as 'sick' since they are unsure how to behave as 'old' (Blau, 1973). Bengston's presentation of social reconstruction takes the assumptions of labelling theory and suggests possible inputs (such as providing alternative interpretations and evaluations, building up adaptive problem solving, providing improved material conditions) to encourage the development of a more positive self-view. This is an attractive presentation in so far as it offers a practical prescription for action but some of the assumptions are, as has been suggested earlier, questionable. Not all older people, for instance, have a negative self-concept (Brubaker and Powers, 1976).

Understanding ageing: individual perspectives
The majority of approaches that have so far been presented have assumed that ageing is open to being understood on the basis of scientific study and within the context of social phenomena: it is assumed that the effects of ageing can be measured. Some mention has been made of the subjective feelings of the older person and the importance of understanding them through a knowledge and exploration of group and individual biographies. The implicit

basis of the majority of gerontological approaches has an interest
in improving the quality of individual and social life for older
people. Novak (1979) has argued that this model of gerontology –
which he calls liberal social gerontology – contains assumptions
which actually frustrate longer term goals for older people. The
alternative approach he proposes is primarily existentialist and
stresses the ability of the individual to reformulate his experience as an acting human being. He argues that 'modern liberal
social science has produced a version of successful ageing that
requires the intervention of the state in processing the population to produce "the greatest good of the greatest number".'
His response is that we should learn from older philosophies 'the
capacity to reformulate society "in spite of" physiological infirmity and old age.'

Another view which may be important in understanding how
each individual experiences old age focuses on the meaning of
time. In one sense this can be linked to the earlier discussion of
Erikson's concept of ego-development and the life cycle: only in
old age is it possible to experience a personal sense of the over-
all life cycle. Butler (1975) points out that old age is the only
period of life with no future and that older people begin to emphasize the quality of the time remaining rather than the quan-
tity. A study of 120 residents in institutions for older people
found that their awareness of 'finitude' (their estimate of time
remaining before death) was a better predictor of disengagement
than chronological age; those high in awareness of limited time
before death were low on activity count (Sill, 1980). It is common to talk of time as an objective property: older people have
more time, time on their hands, etc., and time is a commodity to
be spent. But another view of time stresses the subjective experience and meaning. There is little or no evidence that the
meaning of time to older people is any different than its meaning to younger people. It is hard not to speculate, however, that
an hour in the life of an isolated, lonely old lady is not more significant to her than it is to the busy doctor or social worker with
whom she may spend that hour. Using a case study of a London
Day Centre, Hazan (1980) attempts to show that the life of older
people outside the Centre is so alienated and unsatisfying that
they create an experience of timelessness or limbo state in the
centre and reinforce that experience with a series of group mechanisms.

From the perspective of man taking an active part in constructing his view of the world it may be possible to pursue a more
holistic view of ageing. Ageing is a process and it is possible to
set up and scientifically 'measure' theoretical explanations of
phenomena which are observed during that process. However, to
regard these observations and theories as knowledge is risky.
Understanding the experience of ageing requires an awareness of
how people take an active part in constructing their experience.

How, then, do older people feel about ageing? The academic
and professional literature about ageing has grown rapidly in

recent years but with one or two outstanding exceptions there
have been few contributions to gerontology from older people
themselves. There is, of course, a rich source of ideas and
attitudes in literature, biographies, history and memoirs, and an
excellent review of the history of some of these is available (Freeman, 1980). A series of conversations with older people reported
by Seabrook (1981) also makes very helpful and illuminating read-
ing. Within gerontology, however, much of the material available
for discussion is concerned with how younger people feel about
old age and much is rather speculative. Meares (1975) argues that
society's attitude to older people is inconsistent because we have
two conflicting psychological reactions which he summarizes in
the two phrases: 'He is an old fool; take no notice of him' and
'He is a wise old man; let us listen to what he says.' The negative view of old age has led many writers to present a gloomy
pessimistic view, but the positive views do exist.

Gladys Elder has written passionately about the position of
older people and when herself old, and in poor health wrote: 'Let
us face it: except for a fortunate minority, old age *is* intolerable,
it *is* an invincible, inexorable enemy. Face this and we have taken
the first step towards making it more tolerable' (1977, p. 41).

At the age of 80 Margery Fry made a similar point:

Ah! here I come to the real sting of declining years, that sight
and hearing, movement and even mind itself may depart before
death comes. Moreover, for those who escape such deprivation
the dread of it too often lies like a shadow over years that
would otherwise be happy (1954, p. 11).

For the older person the fear or the reality of physical or intellectual decline is obviously important but there are compensations.
Kathleen Gibberd, also in her eighties, wrote:

Seen from the inside, old age is not merely a downhill process.
In reality it is a very up-and-down affair, rather like a mountain descent where one finds oneself sometimes on a sunny
plateau and then on a new and exhilarating height. Despite the
fact that parts of the body deteriorate, the last phase of life
brings positive advantages (1977, p. 2).

Much of the writing by older people about the personal experience of ageing reflects ambivalence: the dilemma of feeling like
the person they were when younger but locked into a body which
no longer has the same physical capacities or appearance. As
Margery Fry, again, put it:

But it is another of the revelations of coming age that its leisure shows a queer paradox in the nature of time. When we
know that our years are few we want to live them fully, to
make up for the waste of neglected experience. But time plays
us a dirty trick. With our retarded metabolism the days and

weeks seem to race by.... Yet though time on a large scale is
so short, from hour to hour the minutes seem to drag. (1954,
p. 10).

Rosalind Chambers, also aged 84, wrote in a similarly mixed
vein:

Old age is not on the whole pleasant and is generally unat-
tractive both to those who are experiencing it and to those who
have not yet got there. But everyone who survives long enough will have to go through with it. My own philosophy, if
you can call it that, is to go on fighting for as long and as
much as is possible (1980, p. 82).

Both positive and negative views do exist. A survey of the
opinions of younger groups suggested that older people have
'patience, tolerance and an ability to listen (hopefully turning a
blind eye to the impatience and intolerance of so many old
people)' (Age Concern, England, 1974, p. 39). As the earlier
discussion has shown, research does, however, highlight a difference between the generalized and the personalized view of old
age. It seems likely that people will grow old as they have grown
up, in their own individual way in response to their experience
of the environment in which they find themselves and the people
with whom they live and work. It is also likely that for each individual growing old will be a changing, fluctuating experience:
Kathleen Gibberd's 'up-and-down affair'.
A number of surveys have confirmed the importance of subjective perceptions to attitudes in old age. A survey of the problems of old people in Coventry (Coventry Social Services, 1972)
found, for example, a wide-ranging effect of the subjective view
of their health held by the elderly people surveyed; this, it was
felt, was rooted in personality characteristics and differing attitudes to life. Similarly, an action-research project on elderly
people and welfare benefits in Wandsworth (Pensioners' Rights
Project Association, 1978) found that non-claimants of a benefit,
whether or not they had heard of the benefit before the survey,
tended to perceive grounds for claiming it in terms of subjective
feelings of need rather than in terms of any objectively defined
legal entitlement. In relation to health care, Coleman points out
that 'It's what people expect, what people find normal that de-
termines how they react to things, and how satisfied they feel
with their situation' (1979, p. 58).
To the individual growing old and being old is essentially a
personal experience, felt in subjective terms. To quote once more
from Kathleen Gibberd:

So much that once mattered now does not, so much that was
once so serious, now seems laughable. One is on the 'last
stage of an extraordinary journey'. It is a last chance, not to
prove oneself as in youth, but to find one's own aspect of

truth, to see further while there is still light (1977, p. 3).

The existence of stereotypes does, however, have important effects. Stereotypes influence and shape the expectations that
others have of an individual and may also affect the way he sees
himself. The danger for the ageing person is that he may be pres-
sured by stereotyped expectations into acting and living within
limits which are unacceptable to him, that those around him will
not permit him to lead the kind of life he wishes to lead.

Some recent surveys have thrown interesting light on the general position of older people in society. A survey conducted in
1974 for Age Concern England among 2,700 retired people found
that the majority felt that someone relied on them and that those
who felt relied upon were less likely to feel lonely or to be in
poor health. Almost two-thirds of the sample felt that they did
help other people in such ways as baby-sitting, shopping, visiting sick or lonely people, and doing minor house repairs. However, the survey did also find that 8 per cent of the sample were
unable to think of anything that they looked forward to. This
represents a recurring theme in research on the elderly as a
group – the majority of old people are involved closely with other
people in their community by virtue of the services they provide
and receive but nevertheless a substantial minority of old people
do seem to experience old age as time of loss, deprivation and
unhappiness.

Another very important survey conducted by Mark Abrams for
the Age Concern Research Unit (1978) looked at a group of
people aged 75 or over. The survey demonstrates the particular
deprivations of this age group: almost 50 per cent were living
alone; 35 per cent had no living offspring; about 20 per cent
felt acute loneliness. It may be statistically possible to discuss
old age as a time when the majority of people lead a reasonably
satisfied life, closely integrated with family and friends, but
there is little doubt that a substantial minority experience old
age as a time of problems, increasing age being a particularly
important influence. Perhaps the most important finding in
Abrams's survey was that when respondents were asked to describe what they felt made for a satisfying life for people like
themselves the biggest single group of replies was in terms of
'having good neighbours and friends'. Interaction and interdependence is clearly very important to the ways in which
people see their lives. It will be shown later that material resources and good health are very significant in life satisfaction
but the existence of other people to provide support is of primary importance. It is significant that only half of Abrams's
respondents over the age of 75, who described having good
neighbours and friends as essential for a satisfying and pleasant old age, said that they had this to any extent.

In spite of what are objectively inferior conditions in many
aspects of their general life situation it is interesting to note that
older people as a group appear to be generally more satisfied with

their lot in life than younger people. One survey (Abrams, 1977a) found that, on a range of factors, including housing, the district in which they lived, the standard of living, education and leisure, and an over-all life satisfaction, the majority of older people were more satisfied than younger people. The only aspect of their circumstances on which they experienced lower levels of satisfaction than younger groups was their health. Nevertheless it should also be noted that one-fifth of the respondents expressed very low levels of satisfaction not only with life as a whole but also with all the other factors surveyed.

UNDERSTANDING AGEING: REFLECTIONS

It would hardly be realistic to attempt a summary of the approaches discussed so far. What has been offered is in fact a very selective summary of some of the most commonly cited ideas or theories about ageing. The most important theme has been the presentation of a dichotomy: older people can be seen as a group but must also be viewed as individuals. This in turn has implications for practice. It may be true to argue that there is no such thing as old age, only individual people each at a point in the ageing process (Brearley, 1975a) but the individual experience is shaped by attitudes and by the opportunities available. It is necessary to develop policies to make provision for the well-being of all older people as well as to implement strategies within those policies to provide for individuals in need.

For the purposes of this book it would be useful to be able to set down a clear statement of current social values in relation to provision for older people. Only if the outcomes we regard as negative can be identified will it be possible to proceed to detailed plans for the management of hazards which make those dangerous or feared outcomes likely. On a superficial level it would be easy to list unpleasant features of old age: loneliness, bereavement, poor health, disability, inadequate income, etc. In the following chapter some of these kinds of issues will be taken up in detail in relation to hazards. A more careful analysis of society's attitudes to older people, however, illustrates the complexity of attempting to explore values. Values may be found in the over-all policy decisions made about older people and inferences drawn about the principles underlying these decisions. More explicitly they may also be found in decisions made about individual cases during the course of professional practice. At least three groupings of dangers can be explored in the light of what has already been suggested here. There are dangers to society from a sizeable group of older people 'in need' or 'at risk' and linked to this there are dangers to older people associated with being chronologically older. Finally, there are dangers to the ageing individual which arise during the ageing process.

Dangers and the ageing population
The proportion of older people in our society is constantly growing and is likely to continue to do so for some time to come. This
is hardly a new discovery although some writers do seem to introduce it as such. One of the most important post second-world-war
books in the field of care of older people (Howell, 1953) began by
recognizing that the chief characteristic of the latter half of the
twentieth century would be the steady growth in the number of
old people. Twenty-five years later Abrams noted (1977b) that
population projections for the next twenty years estimate a slight
fall in the number aged 60 and over. The number of people between 60 and 74 is expected to decline by 8.5 per cent but over
the same period the number of people over 75 is expected to increase by as much as 23 per cent and the numbrs over 85 will
increase by 42 per cent. The most striking aspect of the ageing
of the population, then, is the considerable proportionate increase in those who might be regarded as the very old. A distinction has sometimes been made between the 'young old' and
the 'old old' and it is in the latter grouping that the growth in
need is most likely to occur.

The development of policy for an ageing population is much
more complex than simply counting the numbers. It will involve
determining 'the place which should be assigned to the aged in
society and the means of ensuring them this place' (Laroque,
1978, p. 267). Macintyre (1977) argues that old age has not always been seen as a problem and the kind of problem it is seen
to be has varied over time. In a rather different form she discusses the ambivalence which has been identified from other
contexts of the study of ageing. She suggests that the amount
of concern expressed about old age and whether it has been perceived as a problem by policy makers has varied considerably in
England. The changes which she identifies in the fashionableness
of old age as a topic of concern are, she argues, due not so much
to any empirical changes in numbers or conditions but to changes
in perceptions of those numbers and conditions. She further proposes that there have been changes in the sort of problem old
age has been considered to be and distinguishes between the
humanitarian and the organizational perspectives. From the
humanitarian perspective, ageing is seen as problematic because
it brings suffering and costs for older people: action in this
sense is in terms of ameliorating or preventing problems by reducing costs to the individual. The organizational perspective,
on the other hand, stresses the burden which old age puts on
society as a whole: action is consequently focused on reducing
the social costs to the community. Applying these concepts to
the risk theme it would seem that the increasing proportion of
older people in society creates dangers in so far as there is an
increased likelihood of cost to the community and an increased
likelihood that larger numbers of older people will experience
ageing in problem terms.

Danger and the problem elderly
There is ample data on which to base a gloomy picture of the
numbers of older people in difficulty. A recent OPCS survey of
people aged 65 and over, for example, provides potentially very
depressing numbers (Hunt, 1978). As many as 30 per cent of
older people are shown to be living alone; nearly 80 per cent of
those living alone are women and over 35 per cent are women
aged 75 or over. The proportion of people living alone increases
to 44 per cent among those over 85 years. Although nine out of
ten of the total sample are able to go out without assistance,
less than half of those aged 85 and over are able to do so. Including those who are bedfast or house-bound, nearly three-
fifths have some kind of disability, this proportion rising from
just over half among those between 65 and 74 to over three-
quarters of those aged 85 and over. Of the whole elderly population, one-quarter consists of widowed people living alone and
one-third of them will have done so for at least ten years. About
5 per cent of all old people are never visited by relatives and
over 5 per cent say they have no close living relatives.

   Abrams's survey of the over 75s (Abrams, 1978) offers similar
opportunities to construct a pessimistic picture of old age. Almost half of those surveyed were living alone and of these almost
four-fifths were widows or widowers and almost all the others
were women who had never married. Some of those who had children had outlived them so that, at the time of the survey, 35 per
cent had no living offspring.

   It is hard to feel cheerful about such numbers presented in
this form and some obvious dangers emerge: being old brings
the likelihood of being alone, of being without the support of
children or family, or of being disabled to some degree. But it is
possible to look at the same figures from a different perspective.
From Hunt's survey, 'The Elderly at Home', (1978) we can see
that seven out of every ten older people do live in shared households and more than half of those aged 85 and over do live with
at least one other person. As many as nineteen out of twenty
have a close relative living and one-third can expect to be visited
by a relative several times a week; almost four out of every five
visit relatives regularly. Similarly, taking Abrams's (1978) results,
over half the very old are not living alone and about three-
quarters of those with living children can expect to see at least
one child once a week or more.

   One major danger in reviewing social policies for old age, in
other words, lies in over-reacting to the difficulties experienced
by some older people and making generalized assumptions that
because some older people have problems then all older people
have similar problems. One qualification of this point is that, although at any point in time only a minority of older people are
experiencing problems and using services, an increasing number
of people can expect to do so at some time in their lives, probably with increasing age.

   One implication of this discussion is that the discussion of policy must focus not only on the problem minority but also on the over-all situation of all older people. In 1978 the government discussion paper 'A Happier Old Age' (DHSS/Welsh Office, 1978) included a foreword by the then Secretaries of State which proposed three aims of policy for 'the older generation, their role in society and the kind of help they need from society'. These aims were, first, to ensure that retirement does not mean poverty; second, to keep people active and independent in their own home and where they have had to go into hospital to get them back into their own home as soon as possible; and, third, to enable older people to take their own decisions about their own lives, 'they must have the fullest possible choice and a major say in decisions that affect them.' Included in these aims are some important value statements which have influenced both policy and practice with older people. In particular the stress on independence and choice is important to practice and these points will be developed later in the book. It should be recognized here that such principles for practice are dependent in operation on a policy which ensures a minimum quality of life for all older people.

Once we try to proceed beyond the basic principles of choice, independence, quality of life, etc., discussion is complicated by the tendency to confuse the concept of 'needs' with that of 'rights'. Perhaps some of the confusion relates to Macintyre's distinction between the humanitarian and organizational views. When we come to consider the issue of preventive services for that group of old people who find old age a time of problems the evaluation of effectiveness or success combines judgments not only about how far services meet needs for individual cases but also about how far they contribute to conserving resources. It seems likely that the best way to prevention and a choice of life-styles is through a broader base of provision for all older people – creating better accommodation, income, health and leisure facilities – as a foundation for provision of health and welfare services for older people with problems (Brearley, 1980).

Dangers arising during the ageing process
So far the discussion has been concerned with costs and outcomes which most people would regard as negative. Throughout the life process individuals are likely to encounter events and possibilities which they themselves will regard as dangers but which may or may not be dangers in the view of others. To take a simple example, we know that some people look forward to retirement while others dread it and we also know that many people do not find that the actual experience of retirement bears much relationship to their expectations. For some people, therefore, retirement is a danger, for others it is not. People are affected differently by different events during their lives. It is possible, however, to identify some aspects as being of pressing concern. Mental infirmity, for example, is an issue of growing importance in the care of older people. Of the population over 65 years of

age, 10 per cent are affected by dementia, about half of these experience severe symptoms; between 1977 and 1995 it is predicted that the number of people aged 80 and over among whom dementia reaches its peak incidence of more than one in five people will expand by over half a million to 1.76 million in England and Wales (Office of Health Economics, 1979). Disability presents a problem of even greater proportions; altogether there are said to be some 800,000 severely disabled people of whom half a million are aged 75 and over and another 1,600,000 are moderately disabled (Disability Alliance, 1979).

Some of the more important hazards presented by the ageing process and faced in old age will be reviewed in the next chapter. For the present purposes it will be enough to conclude by recognizing that the basic value position in relation to older people in society remains reasonably constant. There is, for example, no substantial reason to doubt that most people would have agreed 20 years ago and will agree in 20 years time that independence, self-determination, protection, and adequate provision for the basic necessities of life are essential for older people. What has changed and is constantly changing is what we are willing to regard, and can afford to regard, as 'adequate' provision in the meeting of need. The practical expression of changes in the level of provision will be reviewed in later chapters in an attempt to explore the margins of safety as they are expressed in actual decisions made about older people at risk.

2 AGEING AND VULNERABILITY

Vulnerable literally means capable of being wounded or susceptible to injury. It is a word which is often used in relation to older people and it is clearly a risk-related word; the vulnerable person is one for whom loss or damage is a possibility. Taken to the extreme, in this definition everyone is vulnerable since everyone has something to lose. In practice, the term vulnerability seems to be used to mean that there is a greater likelihood of loss or damage for some people. In the case of older people this includes at least two elements: they are statistically more likely than younger people to experience certain kinds of losses, and they are less well equipped for both physical and social reasons to defend themselves against some losses or dangers.

For the purpose of this discussion a distinction will be made between the idea that older people as a group are more vulnerable than younger people in both these senses, and the suggestion that some older people are much more likely to be endangered than others in specific respects. This distinction between the vulnerable group and endangered individuals is a precarious one which depends on relative probabilities; some factors predispose all older people to danger while others make it more likely that some will suffer the feared outcome. However, the distinction provides an opportunity to distinguish some of the more general factors from specific hazards.

The distinction, therefore, is between older people as a vulnerable group, i.e. people for whom specifiable dangers are a possibility as a consequence of recognizable hazards, and older people who are endangered, i.e. those individuals for whom danger is imminent and/or serious.

WHAT MAKES OLDER PEOPLE A VULNERABLE GROUP?

Some problems arise from things people are actually exposed to in their current situation including environmental pressures such as accommodation and housing, family stress, etc. Other problems arise from exposure to loss and further hazards are associated with lacks or deficiencies in the environment: lack of money, lack of support, etc.

Deficiency hazards

Probably the most commonly identified difficulty is poverty: older people are said to be poor people. This does, however, need careful examination, since not all older people are poor. A full discussion is available in Peter Townsend's major study of poverty (1979), which outlines the finding that a relatively high proportion of the population in the oldest age group live in poverty and explores some of the explanations for this. Some central points can be mentioned here.

Actual income figures, of course, are changing rapidly and therefore have little meaning. In a 1974 study Hewitt argues that the majority of pensioners fall into a very small income range and that three groups can be roughly identified: 'a third who receive supplementary pensions; a third who pay income tax; and a third "in between" (who in fact include an unknown number who would be eligible for supplementary pensions, but who do not claim)' (1974, p. 10).

In his survey of over 75s Abrams (1980) noted that almost 90 per cent of those in that age group relied on the state pension as the main source of income, with a small minority of men (12 per cent) giving their private pension as the main source and an even smaller number of women (5 per cent) naming income from investments and savings. Townsend notes striking differences in the distribution of the elderly and non-elderly around what he calls the 'state's standard of poverty': 20 per cent of older people compared with 7 per cent of younger people were living in poverty with another 44 per cent compared with 19 per cent living on the margins of poverty. Drawing from his own survey material and partly from secondary sources, Abrams (1980) also notes that in most elderly households the average income per equivalent adult is some 15 to 20 per cent below that in households where the head is an employed person. Older people are therefore more likely than younger people to have low and inadequate incomes: Townsend suggests that this is primarily related to their heavy dependence on social-security incomes derived from the state and their separation from access to alternative sources of income - particularly to paid employment.

All the findings stress the heavy reliance of older people on state-derived income and it is also apparent that at present income decreases with increasing age. Among those aged 75 and over the gross weekly household income is 30 per cent lower than among those between 65 and 69 years old (Abrams, 1980). Townsend's basic hypothesis is that poverty in old age relates to two factors: the low levels of resources and restricted access to resources relative to younger people. This is related in turn, he argues, not only to the heavy reliance on state pensions but also to the fact that the resources held by many old people fail to keep their value in comparison to the resources of other groups, as well as to the greater exposure of older people to loss (of spouse or other family, retirement, decay of accommodation, etc.)

which also tends to deprive them of access to secondary resources.

Hewitt (1974) also suggests several reasons for the increase of poverty with old age. She argues that many of the very elderly had little or no chance to save when they were younger; and the needs of the very old may be higher (special diets, adaptations to the home, help with housework, etc.). She also suggests that poverty in retirement has its roots in the economic oppression of women. Since two-thirds of pensioners are women, the fact that some women outlive their husbands whose pension or earnings may die with them is obviously important. Similarly a relatively high number of women amongst today's very elderly population have never married and the relatively low level of women's wages and the widespread exclusion of women from occupational pension schemes is also a major influence. Poverty in old age, like old age itself, is predominantly a female experience.

Quoting government survey sources, Abrams (1980) makes the important point that in households where the head is a retired person 57 per cent of all expenditure is taken up in meeting the basic necessities of existence: housing, fuel and food. Further, he notes that in order to meet these basic needs older people have to make severe economies in other aspects of life - economies on footwear and clothing, on durable consumer goods, on transport and on services. Interestingly, he also notes that in the average pensioner household the expenditure on food and the quantities of food consumed are higher than in the average British household. An important implication of these findings is that poverty of old age seems to express itself not so much in the meeting of basic survival needs but in relation to the broader aspects which contribute to a quality of life. Old age is, for many, a question of economic survival.

Developing this point a little, Abrams (1980) found that, although the majority of the over 75s said they had no need of extra income if they were to live without any money worries and in reasonable comfort, 43 per cent said that they could only do so with more money. Again this was generally related to the need for basics - heating, food and clothing. One in fourteen also claimed to be unable to make ends meet on the resources they had. Equally importantly, only three-fifths of Abrams's respondents felt that their present income gave them security for the future.

The general picture confirms:

1 that older people are on average poorer than younger people.
2 although there is a wide range of incomes among older people, the majority cluster in a relatively small income band and the great majority are primarily reliant on state provision.
3 income currently decreases with increasing age.
4 income is devoted mainly to the basic necessities of survival.
5 a substantial minority feel their income is inadequate for comfort and two in every five do not feel their income provides security for the future.

Finally, Townsend notes the fact that life-long occupational status is a major influence on poverty in old age. Low occupational status (linked with father's low status) is associated with poverty in old age. He also identifies the paradox that, although public opinion apparently favours substantial improvements in the income of older people, government intervention does not seem to match the generosity of that opinion. He argues that the underlying failure may not be simply lack of provision but an inadequacy of explanation for the failure; if we do not explain the lack then we cannot understand the persistence of the problem (1979).

A second important deficiency for many older people is the lack of close supporting family or friends. Of people over 65 years of age, 30 per cent live alone, nearly 37 per cent live with an elderly spouse only and a further 7 per cent with a non-elderly spouse. The likelihood of living alone increases with increasing age: 25 per cent of those aged between 65-74 live alone and this proportion increases to 37 per cent among those aged 75-84 and 44 per cent of those over 85 years of age (Hunt, 1978). Abrams's (1978) survey of people over 75 years found that almost half were living alone. In both of these surveys women are shown to be far more likely than men to be living alone: this is primarily associated with the fact that they are more likely than men to live to be older.

Being alone is not necessarily a negative experience; many people, at all ages, choose to live alone. However, it has been recognized for a long time that being alone predisposes to isolation. Isolation is a complex concept and is difficult to measure with accuracy since the feeling of isolation or otherwise is as likely to be as important to the individual as any objective sum of contacts. Abrams constructed an index of isolation which included factors relating to living alone: attendance at clubs, churches, etc.; contact with family; and contact with other supporting people. From this rough scale almost one-quarter were identified as 'isolates' but only a very small percentage registered extreme isolation and as many as 44 per cent were leading relatively active and gregarious lives. Notably, it was found that among older people living with others, comparatively large minorities had only limited outside contacts (Abrams, 1978).

In a government survey, conducted in 1976, it was found that 15 per cent of older people (including the bedfast and housebound) never visit relations or friends, but this proportion rises to 39 per cent of those over 85. Only one older person in fifty neither receives nor makes any visits. Less than half of all older people attend social centres. This survey makes it clear that it is the house-bound and bedfast who are the most severely isolated, while those over 85 and those who are divorced are also likely to be isolated (Hunt, 1978).

One factor which has been said to be important in predicting isolation is geographical separation from family. In the great majority of cases this does not seem to be a major factor, although in a minority of situations it plays some part. Clearly family and close friends are of primary importance in providing social contact and support for older people and those people who are isolated tend to be more likely to be those who have never had children or whose children have died. Statutory or voluntary social workers play a relatively small part and have no contact at all with the great majority of older people. It should also be remarked that retirement migration, which was once assumed to create problems for the surviving partner in a marriage, is less problematic than has been suggested. Some older people do regret moving, but for the majority it seems to work out reasonably well (Karn, 1977).

Living alone is by no means a universal experience in old age, nor is isolation. But the likelihood of both increases substantially with ageing. In so far as each may be regarded as negative by the individual who experiences them they are dangers, but more importantly they introduce and increase the likelihood of loneliness. This will be reconsidered later.

General hazards
Retirement creates hazards in a number of respects. It has already been argued that the pressure to leave full-time employment at a fixed chronological age separates older people from access to the opportunity to earn. Retirement first and foremost creates income loss.

As the single age-related change which is likely to affect almost all people either directly or indirectly, retirement has been the subject of considerable study. The available studies of attitudes to retirement have tended to concentrate on attitudes to the choice between work and retirement. When they approach retirement, workers commonly give as their reason for retiring either 'ill health' or 'work too tiring', with 'compulsory retirement' also as a common reason (Shanas et al., 1968). Work by Jacobson (1972) suggests that the majority of workers would prefer a flexible system of retirement rather than complete retirement. This study also stresses the importance of ill health as a reason for retirement among workers in 'heavier', physically demanding occupations. A study by Crawford (1972) also suggests that the extent of activity and involvement outside the immediate work situation has an influence on attitudes in the immediate period before retirement; this tends to involve social-class factors. Over all, there is some evidence that a proportion of workers would wish to remain in employment at least on a part-time basis. Jacobson (1972) found 63 per cent would have wished to do so and in the cross-national study of Shanas et al. (1968) 32 per cent gave 'forced to retire' as the reason for retirement.

Obviously there is a difference between viewing retirement negatively and wanting to continue in work. Nevertheless it seems likely that some people enter the retirement period unwillingly. The cross-national study found that a substantial proportion of people in Britain who had been retired less than three years said they wished to work: the length of time in retirement seems to be influential in this. Over all, good health and level of income seem to be significant factors in whether or not the retirement period is regarded positively.

Although there does seem to be evidence that older workers would wish to continue working there is also, paradoxically, pressure towards earlier retirement. Phillipson (1978) associates this primarily with the emergence of unemployment as a major problem in capitalist economies but also argues that pension arrangements will be an increasingly important element in trade-union bargaining. Improvements in pensions, he suggests, will be a crucial element in confirming the trend towards a more positive concept of retirement. Phillipson's approach to building a theoretical proposition in this field is a welcome one but the dilemma remains. Many older workers view retirement with apprehension and, particularly in the immediate post-retirement years, they wish to continue working: yet there is also a pressure to earlier retirement.

This may be partly a reflection of changing attitudes to work and leisure which are currently in some confusion. Older people are provided with time to rest and enjoy leisure by retirement from work but many of them are excluded from the income necessary to such enjoyment because they can no longer work. Retirement therefore brings income loss, role loss and separation from those significant activities which gave meaning and identity to many in the work situation, and brings not leisure time, but 'time on their hands'.

This position should not be exaggerated. A study by Age Concern of 2,700 people of pensionable age considered the attitudes of the retired. Some 79 per cent did not agree at all that they 'enjoyed being retired at first but after a while got fed up of it'; and only 9 per cent agreed strongly with the statement (1974). The majority of people do express satisfaction with retirement – but it was shown early that a majority of older people express satisfaction with almost everything but their health.

Health changes with ageing have commonly been seen to be inevitable but it is important to separate the effects of the social processes of ageing from the normal biological changes of ageing and the pathological processes of disease (Gray, 1980). Older people have been found to be reluctant to report illness to their doctor and one of the reasons for this is that they attribute their physical changes or deterioration to old age. The positive and optimistic view developed and propounded by progressive physicians in health care of the elderly is that many of the features which have been thought to be the result of ageing are the result of disease. Many functions of the body do deteriorate with age although most organs have a reserve capacity which ensures that age-related changes give rise to symptoms only rarely. Symptoms become apparent when pathology is superimposed on age-related changes (Hall, 1979; see also Chapter 6).

This optimistic view must, however, be seen in the light of lack of training in the special health-care needs of older people and the stereotypical attitudes of many medical personnel who dismiss older people as bothersome or incurable. Good preventive medicine and dealing with the multiple pathology of illness in old age demands a level of skill, time and commitment which many doctors do not possess.

How far, then, is health a problem to older people? Most people say they are in good health for their age yet several studies have found up to three-quarters of older people with at least one unknown moderate or severe disability (Williamson et al., 1964). In later life it is also common for people to suffer from several diseases at once (Agate, 1972). Sensory loss is common: in particular, changes in sight and hearing occur. The most important development during the current century has been in the mastery of the infectious diseases and the increased importance of what Isaacs (1980) has called non-lethal diseases, including atherosclerosis, diabetes, arthritis and dementia. As more people live to be old, so more people are exposed to these diseases. As Isaacs puts it, 'The average age of death creeps ever upward, casting behind it the lengthening shadow of pre-death – the period of life preceding death in which independent existence is not possible' (1980, p. 30).

In relation to their general health, then, older people can expect physiological decline in general functioning and some physical disease processes. Of increasing importance at the present time is mental ill health among older people. Studies in the community have reported that between 41 per cent and 55 per cent of older people at home have some psychiatric disorder (Whitehead, 1974). This does, of course, depend very much on the definition of psychiatric disorder but there seems to be some agreement that dementia is present in some one out of every ten older people, the proportion rising to one in five of those aged over 80. At least 5 per cent of those over 65 in the community suffer from organic psychosis and a further 10 per cent have some functional mental disorder of moderate severity (MIND, 1979).

Four main categories of psychogeriatric illness have been suggested as a basis for service planning (Holford, 1972): first, long-stay patients who have entered hospital earlier in life and have grown old; second, those patients in whom an episode of functional mental disorder presents in old age; third, patients with what is usually called organic brain syndrome; and, fourth, patients with acute confusional states. The social consequences of such illness are obvious: a large number of older people with severe mental illness or dysfunction are cared for in the community by relatives. This creates considerable strain and represents a major concern for caring services.

No clear causal effects of social deprivation in creating mental illness have been found but the possibility cannot be ruled out (De Alarcon, 1971). Studies in Glasgow, for instance, in three

general-practitioner groups suggest several factors which appear
to contribute to deteriorating mental health - feelings of loss and
pointlessness, lack of social life - and some which seem to contribute to positive mental health, including keeping pets, a religious faith, and a reasonable social life (Gilmore, 1976).

The issues relating to physical and mental health are of fundamental importance and each is developed in detail in separate
chapters later in the book.

The government discussion document, 'A Happier Old Age', recognized the importance of good accommodation to older people:
'although most old people live in the community, their ability to
do so can depend as much on the kind of accommodation they
occupy as the support they receive' (DHSS, 1978, p. 26). It is a
conventional wisdom that older people are more likely than
younger ones to be living in sub-standard accommodation and it
is not difficult to find evidence to support this. The reasons for
this position are complex but three particular factors can be highlighted (Butler et al., 1979).

First, older people tend to be living in older houses, which are
less likely to have basic amenities and which tend to be in poorer
condition. In fact, the 1976 OPCS survey (Hunt, 1978) found that
the proportions of older and younger households living in pre-
1919 housing were roughly similar. However, within this finding
there are considerable variations: almost half of older households
in Greater London and three-quarters of private tenants were in
older housing. Older people in council housing are much less
likely to be in older accommodation. Regional variations are obviously important and, as the National Federation of Housing
Associations commented in 1978, information on the housing
needs of the elderly available from the local authorities is too
varied to be of immediate use in deciding precisely what to do
and where (National Federation of Housing Associations, 1978).
There are general indications that housing amenities are more
likely to be lacking among older households (Hunt, 1978) but the
picture is complicated. Among the 65 to 74 years' age group,
housing is little different from younger groups but disparities
increase with age.

This is partly linked to the second basic reason for less adequate housing among older people which is that they are more
likely to be in privately rented accommodation. Although the proportion of householders who own their own homes (either outright or with a mortgage) is roughly similar in older and younger
groups the former are much more strongly represented among
tenants (31 per cent council, 17 per cent private compared with
18 per cent and 6 per cent of younger households (Hunt, 1978)).

Finally, the burden of home ownership in terms of maintenance
costs for older people with limited incomes leads to deterioration
of some properties.

A rich source of material on attitudes to housing older people
(and on attitudes to many other aspects) is available in the many

and varied responses to the discussion document 'A Happier Old Age' (DHSS, 1978). Although all of the responses are agreed on the importance of housing, a number make special comments. The Beth Johnson Foundation (1978), for instance, comments that the lack of basic amenities experienced by some older people may be generally unacceptable but that some older people may still resist change. The need for owner occupiers to contribute to improvement costs and for tenants to face the disruption of moving may lead to an acceptance of lower standards as a less disturbing alternative. The Personal Social Services Council response (1978) confirms these points.

The National Federation of Housing Associations (1978) view was that there should be a wide range of housing choice available to the elderly so that their ability to remain independently in the community is not constrained by lack of opportunity. Similarly, the Disability Alliance (1979) stress the importance of flexibility of housing and in particular the need to relax the transfer policies of many local authorities. This organization also notes the particular problems of inner-city and retirement areas and suggests that experience has shown that in such areas other people are more likely to be isolated and impoverished because family living standards will fall relatively, if not absolutely. It therefore proposes that 'the best "preventive" policy for the elderly is by means of a positive economic, industrial and employment policy' (p. 40).

Older people, then, are more likely to be in poorer accommodation with fewer amenities; they are more likely to be tenants; and owner occupiers encounter problems of maintenance costs and also problems relating to the fact that their capital is often tied up in housing and cannot be released for other uses. Once again, however, there is no uniform picture and the conditions vary widely. A number of important arguments remain to be explored about the role of specialist housing – sheltered accommodation, granny-annexes, residential homes, etc. These will be taken up again later. For the present purposes it is enough to note that the general accommodation picture confirms the vulnerability of older people. In order to begin to overcome some of the pressing issues, the National Corporation for the Care of Old People (1978) response to 'A Happier Old Age' calls for priority to be given to improving the housing of the over 75s; for the requirement of published assessments of the housing needs of the elderly by local authorities; and for making older non-residents and home owners eligible for local authority housing. Without such changes, inadequate housing remains a hazard to many older people.

Hazards and loss
Much has been written and discussed about old age as a time of loss: 'ageing presents the individual with a number of loss situations each of which has to be compensated for in some way'

(Brearley, 1975a). It should be clear from what has already been written here that this is a realistic comment. Older people are likely to lose work roles and associated income; they lose physical abilities and sometimes their physical and mental health; and they lose family and friends through death. Not all older people are affected by all of the major loss situations. Some may be only minimally affected whilst others may experience severe losses. The majority of people do seem to adapt to the changes which ageing and old age bring, on the basis of learned or reserve capacities, and with the help of family support or the support of friends. Only for a minority will losses bring insurmountable problems or ones which require the help of formal helping services. Some losses, however, are more universally experienced than others.

Loss of mobility has been identified as a particular problem. 'A Happier Old Age' (DHSS, 1978) focuses its concern about mobility primarily on issues of transport but mobility difficulties are much broader than this might suggest. Mobility has been defined as the freedom to move about without restriction (Robson, 1978). Restrictions on mobility may relate both to the availability of transport and to the limitations on the individual caused by his own impairment (e.g. frailty, poor eyesight, etc.)
Walking is a particularly important means of getting about for older people. In Britain walking accounts for 39 per cent of journeys made by the average person but among the over 65s this increases to 53 per cent (quoted in Robson, 1978). Not surprisingly the ability to walk and to get out of the house decreases with age. In a survey of handicapped and impaired people in Britain (Harris, 1968) between 8 per cent and 11 per cent of people surveyed in nine areas were found to be bedfast or housebound. In the more recent survey of the elderly at home (Hunt, 1978), a lower figure of 4.5 per cent was found. This survey suggests that up to the age of 84 the great majority of people do not have any difficulty getting out of doors but that age marks a noticeable deterioration shown particularly in the need for help in going out. One factor in limiting mobility, therefore, is health status – frailty, illness or disability.
Commenting on 'A Happier Old Age', Age Concern, England suggest that transport and mobility represent 'an area of great concern to elderly people and one which, if the services and conditions are not sympathetically applied, will have bandwagon effects on other social policies' (1978, p. 10). It has been increasingly recognized that public-transport practices must take account of the needs of the elderly. Age Concern, England raise two issues in particular: since older people are more likely to be walking and are more vulnerable to accidents on the road (the accident rate among pedestrians over 60 years is 1.5 times that of the rest of the adult population (DHSS, 1978)) pedestrian facilities, especially road crossings, should take account of this need. The other major issue they suggest is that of concessionary

fares. This is particularly important since only a minority of older people have a car: this relates to the expense, the difficulties of driving which increase with age, and lack of driving experience (Robson, 1978). Finally, an important aspect of mobility is ease of access to buildings. This is particularly necessary in essential buildings such as shops, hospitals, doctors surgeries, chemists, etc.

Limited mobility contributes to the vulnerability of older people and rests on three basic reasons: the lack of access to car transport; the fact that limited income restricts the use of all forms of motorized transport; and the influence of poor health is important. Nevertheless, age is a less important factor than income and health (Robson, 1978) which, as has also been shown in relation to satisfaction in retirement, are most important considerations for many older people.

The one loss which we can all expect to encounter is the loss of life. It does not seem appropriate to consider death itself as a danger or the possibility of death as hazardous since it is the one certainty in an uncertain world. Indeed, the reduction in mortality rates which has led to the increasing numbers of people living to old age means that it is more appropriate in some senses – as we have seen earlier – to regard increasingly large numbers of old people as the more important danger. Death may not be a danger in an abstract sense but it may represent danger in two practical senses. Some people will feel anxious at the prospect of dying and, second, the more important danger is not death itself but the manner of dying.

Reactions to the prospect of dying seem to vary widely. For some older people death may be a less forbidding prospect than it was when they were younger while for others it may create anger, frustration, anxiety, or confusion (Bromley, 1974). Some older people apparently accept the prospect of their death in a matter of fact way and for those around them this may be the least painful alternative. Butler (1963) suggests that those who have always tended to be future-orientated in their attitudes may be especially prone to despair while those who have caused injury to other people may experience guilt. He argues generally that the degree to which people see the approach of death as a crisis varies with the individual personality. Significantly he points out that, although the predominant image of a 'good death' is one of calm and dignity he does not 'intend to imply that a "serene and dignified acceptance of death" is necessarily appropriate, noble, or to be valued. Those who die screaming may be expressing a rage that is as fitting as dignity' (p. 74). Bromley also confirms the suggestion that personality or typical forms of adjustment in other, earlier aspects of life are likely to influence the response to death (1974).

It has been argued, however, that an older person who contemplates his own death will be aware that he will suffer various losses including loss of self (loss of body and sensory awareness);

loss of roles and opportunities to have experiences; and loss of others (Kalish, 1976). While death itself may not be a danger, then, the anticipation of death may contribute to general vulnerability. Further, increasing physical deterioration may accentuate anxieties about the manner of dying. Usually what people seem to fear is not death itself but the pain which they anticipate may attend the actual dying (Hinton, 1967). Two factors which seem to be especially important among those people who do not express fear of dying are good health and spiritual trust: having a religious faith (Papalia et al., 1973).

Older people are vulnerable to death but primarily in the sense that death is more likely to be imminent for them. They are, however, exposed in a number of ways to the danger of dying in an unpleasant manner – perhaps in pain, in distress, or alone. A study of adults in the last year before death, for instance, noted that 'one of the most disconcerting findings was the high proportion of symptoms for which no one had been consulted' (Cartwright et al., 1973). The authors noted the reluctance to mention unpleasant smells and loss of bladder control to the GP either because of fear or embarrassment. Few people die unexpectedly and for most people the last year of life is a time when they suffer a variety of unpleasant symptoms, are restricted and need help with their disabilities. Among those over 65 the proportion of people living alone before death increases with age from one in eight among those 65 to 69 to one in four of those aged 80 or more (Cartwright et al., 1973).

One final aspect should be noted: some people choose to die. The level of suicide is highest among the over 65s for many reasons. And as Dame Eileen Younghusband has asked: 'Does the right to live have as its mirror image the right to die?' (1978, p. 16). Perhaps an important danger is that some people are not able to die when they choose to do so.

This discussion has identified some – though by no means all – of the more general hazards to which people are more likely to be exposed as they age. At this stage two key factors should be noted. First, age measured chronologically is often a less significant variable in determining risk than other elements. Particularly influential are the level of income and the quality of the individual's physical or mental health. Whether or not people find the post-retirement period satisfying is largely dependent on adequate income and good health. Similarly the ability to get out and about and therefore to maintain or develop social contacts is dependent more on income and health than on chronological age. The relationship between needs and housing is also closely bound up with level of income (for instance, in meeting the cost of maintenance and repairs) and with health (in relation, for example, to use of stairs). The second factor follows from these examples: it is not usually realistic to consider one hazard or deficiency in isolation from the many others which are likely to be related to it and to compound its effect. Limited income, for example, contributes to the possibility of failure to meet basic survival needs for food and warmth and this in turn contributes to the deterioration of health which in its turn leads to increasing special need and therefore the need for more income. Older people are not only exposed to specific hazards; they are more likely to acquire a collection of related difficulties. One or two hazards may be well within the coping capacity of the ageing person and his family but what has been called the 'cluster of circumstances' (Saul, 1974) - the coming of a number of simultaneous changes - is likely to create excessive strain and much increased risk.

In spite of these comments it must still be recognized that increasing age brings increasing likelihood of negative consequences. It is that group of people over the age of 75 who are likely to need the support and help of health and social services for many of the reasons outlined here. If this is true of the over 75s, then it is even more true of the over 85s and it is this group which is likely to show the greatest proportionate increase during the next two decades. Ageing, in very general terms, can be closely linked to increasing vulnerability but it is also clear that some older people are more likely than others to experience loss or damage. The reasons for this are, again, very complex and variable but some attempt can be made to pick out significant features.

WHAT MAKES SOME OLDER PEOPLE MORE ENDANGERED THAN OTHERS?

Mention has been made earlier of the importance of the subjective meaning of an experience and it is useful to distinguish between the objective fact that a hazard exists and the subjective meaning of that fact to the person who experiences it. As was suggested in Chapter 1, one view regards older people as passive experiencers of a series of events which determine the course of their lives. More positively, however, they can be seen as taking an active and self-determining part in defining and shaping the way they live their lives. There are clearly factors which interfere with the individuals' capacity to influence the course of events but two dimensions must be taken into account. First, the individual is usually an active influence on events and, second, the individual plays a significant role in defining events for himself.

The implications of this for the practical situation are fundamental. At its simplest level the point may be illustrated in the fact that some people continue to function adaptively in the face of objective circumstances in which others succumb. Examples are easy to come by. In a general sense we have seen already that older people as a group appear to have lower expectations than younger groups: they are satisfied with objectively less adequate services and facilities. There is reason, however, to doubt whether this is a primarily age-related phenomenon. It seems probable that the current generation of 'old old' people have experienced the world in a way in which future generations of older people have not. It is possible that the next generation of older people, more accustomed to demanding and getting services as of right, will be more complaining and more demanding.

More specifically, expectations of health among older people tend to be low. As shown earlier, they tend not to report symptoms of disease to the health services, perhaps because of a belief that old age and illness inevitably go together. Older people minimize their symptoms and they too readily accept them as their lot (Hodkinson, 1980). The hazard may therefore be not only the disease itself but the failure of the individual to recognize it as disease and therefore seek treatment.

Another commonly quoted example is the response to relocation from one form of accommodation to another. In a study of reactions to admission to institutional living it was suggested that those effects on older people usually identified as the result of institutional living are more attributable to reactions to the waiting period before admission (Tobin and Lieberman, 1976). These reactions are attributed to the 'loss meaning of separation' and the feeling of being abandoned and the expected separation. The relationships of older people who are waiting for admission to institutional living with those around them are characterized by feelings of separation and rejection and of being abandoned. Other studies have also confirmed that the element of felt-rejection is important in adjustment following admission to institutional care (Yawney and Slover, 1973). Studies of housing for older people have found similar responses. A study of older people entering age-segregated housing in the United States suggested that either special housing or community-dispersed housing can be satisfactory for the older person who feels he has freely made the choice to move (Sherman, 1975).

An important aspect, then, is how the individual is prepared to perceive the hazard. The key point is that the determination of some people to continue fighting, as Rosalind Chambers (1980) put it, may be a strength which counteracts the effects of some of the hazards. For others depression, apathy or lack of emotional support may compound the individual's reaction and emphasize the effect of the hazards.

With these considerations in mind some further dimensions can be pursued. The concept of strain has been used as a term describing the build up of pressure and stress in the lives of older people and their families (Isaacs, et al., 1972). Help for older people is several times more likely to be provided by a spouse, children or other relatives than it is by any form of organized service. In personal-care tasks relatives are almost always more important than health or social service workers and older people prefer to take their worries to relatives (Age Concern, 1974). It has sometimes been assumed that families do not wish to care for their older relatives but the great bulk of empirical, professional and impressionistic literature suggests that this is not usually the case. Most older people do things for others and have things done for them in return. Some older people are, of course, determinedly independent and a rigid adherence to the principle of maintaining independence does have dangers. I have suggested elsewhere that the enthusiasm for the older person's right to independence - important though that is - should not blind us to their right to be dependent: to interact with and be supported by others. As Professor Olive Stevenson puts it: 'We must commit ourselves to maintaining family ties through support to relatives, forming a partnership between the family and the wider society' (1977, p. 11).

Throughout the twentieth century the percentage of older people in institutional care has remained constant at around 5 per cent (Moroney, 1976) and there is no evidence of wholesale 'dumping' of older people by families. Nevertheless, it is wrong to assume that all older people have access to family life. Abrams (1980) found that among the over 75s over one-third had no living offspring and these people were therefore entirely dependent for companionship on friends and neighbours and rather less significantly on statutory or voluntary social workers. The majority of older people, however, do have contact with families and maintain an important family life and for some this can lead to strain.

One aspect of this is increasing disability. The Disability Alliance have argued that 'the distinctive fact about ageing is the greater likelihood of disablement' (1979, p. 1). Although this is based on a very broad concept of disablement and puts unnecessarily negative stress on physical changes with age, the point is important. The Disability Alliance identify three areas in which particular attention is necessary to provide support for families. First, in the provision of housing; second, in the provision of special income to meet needs arising from disability; and, third, in the development of support services for the care-providers, including weekend relief, holidays, laundry services, etc. Disablement, in other words, can create financial stress, stress relating to inappropriate or inadequate housing, and stress on the carers in the form of both physical and emotional strain.

In reality family stress seems to account for a relatively small proportion of applications for admission to residential care: less than 10 per cent of admissions appear to be attributable to this reason, the majority being related to the inability or anticipated inability of the older person to provide self-care (Brearley et al., 1980). Yet family strain does seem to arise for three main reasons.

First, strain develops for the practical reasons already described: increasing disability, practical dependence and low incomes create pressure for caring families. A further significant point is the growth of the four-generation family. The growing numbers of the 'old old' have led to a situation in which many of the carers are themselves old. When parents are 85 or over their children may well be themselves in retirement.

Second, problems have been identified in relation to the long-standing interactions of families. One study, for example, notes that one-quarter of children report cordial relationships with elderly parents but the remainder report a variety of problems attributed to parental ageing. The children in the study usually tended to relate long-standing intergenerational, or interpersonal problems to the personality structure of the parent (Simos, 1973).

Third, some problems arise as a result of unexpected family events. In a small study of emergency admission into homes for the elderly, Pope (1980) notes three distinct patterns of admission. The largest group was of those dependent on others to provide for the basic necessities of life: for some it was the loss of a caring relative or partner through death or hospital admission, for others it was the result of families finding the burden overwhelming (often as a result of a build up of tension), and for others it was the loss of supporting friends or neighbours which led to admissions. Most importantly this group was admitted not because of any deterioration in themselves but because of a failure of the ability of those who supported them. A second group was much smaller and included those who had been determined to rely on their own resources but for whom illness had created crisis. The third group was characterized by the need for a roof over their heads rather than by any predominant need for care and attention. From this limited evidence there seems to be some support for the proposition that unexpected loss among care-givers is an important hazard to older people.

The question of family strain can be approached slightly differently from the point of view of crisis. One kind of crisis stems from the need to achieve certain developmental tasks. Such tasks exist for the individual but are also relevant to the family. The way in which the family deals with earlier crises may influence later interaction. An obvious example is what has been called the 'middle-age separation crisis' in which middle-aged fathers may be interacting with growing sons at a time when they themselves are vulnerable to job loss, failure in promotion, or threats from younger men at work. Middle-aged mothers may also be made anxious by menopausal changes when daughters are reaching the prime of their sexual years (Wasserman, 1973). If these situations are not adequately dealt with then later problems may occur within the family relationships.

A second view of crisis stresses the importance of unexpected, environmental or personal events. Crisis illness, for example, may have a major impact on family functioning. An older person may find himself suddenly dependent for all his self-care needs, perhaps as a result of a stroke, after being in a position as strong, dependable head of the family. Clearly, this demands substantial readjustment for all the family.

Some more specific hazards can also be identified as contributing to individual risk. Bereavement is of particular significance:

older people are more subject to the loss of those who are close
to them. Grief is not necessarily a problem and a 'normal' process of grieving has been thoroughly described (Parkes, 1972).
For most people bereavement and the consequent grief are dealt
with within the usual family support. For others, however, it
may be associated with longer term feelings of loss, and sometimes with guilt or anxiety and even anger, and the grief may
develop into a true depression rather than be resolved. It is also
possible for bereavement to cause real physical illness and there
is an increase in the death rate in close relatives during the first
year of bereavement (Hall et al., 1978). It is worth remembering,
too, that bereavement is not only related to the loss of a person.
The loss of a limb, or of good health or even of a home may precipitate acute grief reactions or be associated with chronic grieving processes.

A close link has also been drawn between bereavement and
loneliness in old age and the concept of desolation has been used
to refer to the combination of isolation, loneliness and bereavement experienced by some older people (Shanas et al., 1968).
Loneliness is not an easy concept to define since to a large extent it exists in the eye of the beholder. Most definitions seem
to relate the subjective feeling of unhappiness to the recognition
of a need for contact or intimacy with at least one other. One
common aspect seems to be the wish for a specific kind of relationship rather than simply for contact. It is possible, for instance,
to be isolated and lonely amongst a group of people. Plank (1977)
found that almost one-quarter of a sample of residents in residential homes said they neither had a close friend nor chatted
regularly to other residents, and 7 per cent of residents said
they were lonely most days.

Loneliness is more than simply lack of social contacts and
isolation alone is an inadequate predictor. Some approaches to
loneliness stress the role of the individual in creating his own
loneliness. Lake (1980) relates loneliness to a reduced feeling of
self-worth and discusses ways of coping with or curing it which
stress the need for the individual to recognize that it is up to
him to overcome his problem. This kind of approach neglects the
pressures of environmental circumstances, which interact with
self-attitudes. In a consideration of loneliness and rural elderly
in America, Kivett (1979) identified three groups of factors as
being of importance to intervention in loneliness: social activities
and relationships; health and vision; and transportation and communication. This study also stresses the two stumbling blocks to
intervention: the tendency to regard loneliness as deviance and
to suppress our own feelings of loneliness because of the anxiety
they arouse; and, second, the fact that most lonely adults place
the burden of relieving loneliness on others.

Bereavement and loneliness are linked in the feeling of desolation and both are significant features in the breakdown of some
older individuals. What makes desolation and loneliness particularly hazardous is that by definition they seem to imply both a

lack of supporting relationships and a degree of withdrawal or apathy which fosters a self-perpetuating deterioration.

Accidents are a major cause of death and disablement in both men and women over the age of 65 years. In 1971, 4,000 people over that age died in accidents in their own homes (Coni et al., 1980). One type of injury alone, fracture of the neck of the femur accounted in 1974 for an average daily use of 3,070 beds per day by people over 65 (Morfitt, 1979). The majority of accidents result from falls, which are a common hazard among older people. Falls have been classified on the basis of three types of mechanism: accidental falls, such as slipping on ice, tripping on loose carpets, etc.; symptomatic falls resulting from fits or faints, or caused by dizziness; and mixed type falls (Williams, 1979). Many old people have multiple falls and women are particularly vulnerable: they not only have more falls but are more likely to sustain a fractured femur (Hodkinson, 1980). Falls seem to be predominantly the result of genuine accidents but this is in the context of reduced sensory abilities. Impaired adaptation of the eyes to the dark, for example, makes it difficult for older people to go from light to dark at night and increases the hazard in dimly lit homes (Hall et al., 1978). Accidents must also be related to the environment as well as the physical capacities of the individual. Older people in residential homes are particularly vulnerable (Morfitt, 1979).

One aspect of accidents that has attracted particular attention has been the occasional accidental death of older people alone. Such accidents tend to attract a lot of public attention and sometimes statutory services are blamed for not taking better preventive action. One study of people found dead in York shows that it is very difficult to predict such accidents and that there is little evidence of major demand for greater resources on the part of those who were found dead (Bradshaw et al., 1978).

Associated with the increased likelihood of accidents it has also been suggested that older people are more likely to be exposed to violence. Butler (1975) suggests that in the United States older people are victims of violent crime more than any age group. Other authors do not agree with this statement. Cook, writing with others, claims that 'the elderly are the least likely age group to be victimized' and that this is now widely recognized (1978, p. 338). However, it seems clear that older people are more likely to suffer large consequences of crime because they are more frail and are therefore especially harmed by violence and because they have lower incomes and therefore incur relatively greater economic costs. Writing in the British context Mawby and Colston (1979) agree that the elderly may be less vulnerable than younger age groups to crime rather than more so. The over-all picture is variable: the situation in a quiet rural area is likely to be different from an inner-city area. That older people are vulnerable to crime is certain, whether they are more vulnerable than younger people is less sure. This is, of course, of small consolation to those older people who are victims of violence.

The recognition, in the last twenty years, of child abuse as a widespread phenomenon, has led to the development of several perspectives on family violence. The concept of 'granny-bashing' has appeared occasionally in one or two journals and even in more substantial academic works but the evidence that there is any widespread or substantial violence towards older people is very sparse and impressionistic. The few preliminary attempts to consider the subject have made only very limited analysis restricted to the rather trite points that older people bruise easily and identification of abuse is difficult (Renvoize, 1978) and that until recently child abuse was not recognized so we may be on the threshold of recognizing a similar phenomenon among older people (Freeman, 1979). This is not to denigrate these attempts to outline a problem but clearly it is a subject we need much more information about.

Another primarily physical hazard which has been given much attention in recent years is hypothermia. Accidental hypothermia occurs if the temperature of the body care is allowed – unintentionally – to fall below 35°C. The mortality of those with a temperature between 30° and 35°C is about one-third: below 30°C mortality rises to 70 per cent (Coni et al., 1980). It is difficult to find accurate estimates of the incidence of hypothermia since it is often secondary to severe physical disease and those dying at home from hypothermia may not be recognized as such. However, it has been estimated that some 400 to 500 deaths annually in the UK are attributable to hypothermia (Hodkinson, 1980).

Exposure to cold is the most important cause of hypothermia but this is usually coupled with deficiencies in the body's thermoregulatory processes. It is therefore not simply living in cold conditions which is predictive of hypothermia. In a major attempt to identify factors which predispose to hypothermia, Wicks (1978) offers no simple answers to identifying those 'at risk'. He suggests that declining physiology combined with deprived social circumstances are generally predictive. Increasing age is an important factor but Wicks found that many younger pensioners were also at risk. In general, then, people living in cold houses are more at risk but accurate prediction of hypothermia depends on recognition of other physiological and environmental factors and Wicks found no evidence that the cold elderly will identify themselves as such or even that they will ask for help.

Food is one other central element in survival but as the earlier discussion has suggested most older people spend more rather than less than younger people on food. Malnutrition is not common in Britain and surveys have shown that food intake is, on the whole, adequate. The small proportion of older people who are malnourished are likely to be those who are disabled, housebound, and isolated (Brocklehurst, 1978). There are, of course, many other threats to the physical well-being of the individual and this review has not set out to be exhaustive but to outline some of the more important hazards.

Finally, in this review some attention must be given to special groups among the older population. It is perhaps inappropriate to depict women as a special group among the elderly but it has already been stated here that ageing is primarily a female experience. The majority of older people are women: Abrams (1977b) estimates that in 1976 59 per cent of people over the age of 60, and 75 per cent of those over 85, were women.

This creates practical problems, some of which have been outlined already. Women experience poverty more severely than men and, because they survive longer, they are more likely to encounter living alone, bereavement, deteriorating housing, loss of physical abilities and disability, etc. In addition to this Sontag (1972) has written of what she calls the double standard of ageing. She suggests that society offers even fewer rewards for ageing to women than it does to men. Being physically attractive, she argues, is seen as more important for women but beauty, identified with youthfulness, does not stand up to ageing. She also makes a number of similar points about the 'eternal' wisdom of women, which is not seen to increase with age, and the gradual sexual disqualification of women.

In a much more detailed discussion of the social role of older women Matthews (1979) emphasizes the perspective of older women as social actors. She identifies the importance of uncertainty and ambiguity in the place of older women in society. 'Oldness' she identifies as a stigma but because of uncertainty and ambiguity it represents a weak stigma and the position of older women should be seen in this context. A full discussion of the issues relating to the differences between older women and older men is not possible here but stress should be placed on the centrality of the woman's experience of old age.

Elderly ethnic minorities are of growing importance in Britain although relatively little has been written about them. It seems likely that all older people will experience the general hazards outlined here but for some groups additional problems arise. Elderly black people, for instance, may be particularly at risk: they are over-represented in areas of high deprivation, they experience frequent moves and have low incomes. In addition, they face the consequences of immigration and the breaking of family ties; discrimination and prejudice in the host community; tension resulting from the gap between their expectations of Britain and the reality; and the challenge to their accepted view of family care represented by the British concept of care for older people (Pyke-Lees and Gardiner, 1974).

Once again, space does not permit any more than this brief illustration of what is clearly a problem of growing importance. Minority groups of many kinds exist among the elderly and more thought and attention must be given to the impact of general hazards on their special circumstances.

To summarize, a wide range of influences affect whether an individual older person suffers loss or damage. Some basic points have been made.

1 The objective fact of a hazard may be less important than the individual's subjective perception of and response to it.
2 Strain among care-givers is a common feature but most families are prepared to give help to their older relatives.
3 Emergencies and crises sometimes arise as the result of an accumulation of hazards and losses: the cluster of circumstances.
4 Emergencies and crises sometimes arise as a result of the loss of or breakdown of care-givers.
5 Some losses occur as a result of predictable changes while others occur through unpredictable changes. The role of the precipitating factor will be developed in the next chapter.

The discussion here has emphasized the practical nature of hazards in the lives of older people, while recognizing the importance of their reaction to those hazards. Some reference has been made to the importance of personality or earlier learned patterns of behaviours in adaptation to hazards and dangers. Some theoretical positions do focus on the importance of personality in response to risk or problems in old age, but to follow this line places the responsibility for the 'ability to cope', or 'good adaptation' or 'successful ageing' very much on the individual. It has been shown here that many of the pressures on older people derive from social forces which are largely beyond the control of the individual. A strategy for intervention in the total situation of the older person must recognize the interplay of the social context and the individual's adaptive capacity. A more positive and optimistic view is to consider the individual as a consciously self-determinating actor who contributes to the definition and development of his own social world.

3 ACCEPTABLE RISK, ASSESSMENT AND RESOURCES

There is a difference between those risks which are seen to be acceptable because they are within normally recognized limits of reasonableness and those risks which are tolerable. Some people tolerate risks which are unacceptable by normally recognized standards because they are powerless to affect the situation. The fact that an older person lives with risks is therefore no indication of their reasonableness or general acceptability and, as we have seen, many older people have to tolerate high levels of risk in many areas of their lives. Similarly, the concept of fair risk involves slightly different assumptions about the distribution of risks between people and groups. A basic example is the distribution of poverty among the elderly: it is unfair that women should suffer the effects of poverty in old age more than men. It is likely that most people would find it unreasonable or unacceptable that they should do so. But, the paradox continues: older women have to tolerate a higher risk of poverty and society continues to tolerate a situation in which they have to do so.

Recognizing acceptable risk is therefore not only about what is reasonable but also about what is bearable and what is fair. In judging acceptable risk or safety levels, usual practice and recommendations about best available practice give some guide and it may be possible to identify either the minimum level of safety beyond which risks are acceptable or the minimum level of protection beyond which risks are unacceptable. Risk hierarchies may take two forms: those developed for national or regional planning purposes and the personal risk hierarchies used by older people and by those who work with them.

Two particular possibilities for developing an understanding of personal risk hierarchies may be helpful. First, it may be possible to see a hierarchy of individual risk taking based on the difference between basic physiological and safety needs and psychological, self-esteem and self-expression needs. It has already been shown that older people tend to spend their limited income on meeting basic survival needs for food, shelter, and warmth and it seems reasonable to assume that personal priorities will normally focus on this level. Risks to physical well-being and safety are likely to take precedence, although risks to the need for love, friendship and support have also been shown to be of major importance. A second approach to developing an understanding of how individual older people rank risks may be through a combination of outcome probability and outcome evaluation. How, for instance, do older people regard risks of low

probability, but high consequence value? Unfortunately, the
evidence on which to develop such an approach is very limited
at present and this can only be speculative and subjective.

In practice it seems that most decisions about risk and older
people are about risks of high probability and high consequence
– usually high negative consequence. Often the importance of immediate consequence is a key feature of action. The relative
scarcity of resources is a major aspect of assessment: it is not
only a question of what we consider to be a reasonable level of
risk but also of what we can afford to regard as unfair or intolerable. The consequence is that many older people bear a burden
of risk and need which most people would regard as unacceptable
but which society cannot, or will not, reduce. Risk assessment
is, in other words, about the relationship between abilities and
environments, and safety judgments begin with value assumptions
in the real world. As Arie has put it 'A disability in an old person is rarely intelligible except in terms of a balance between
function and setting, and the former can seldom be properly
assessed apart from the latter' (1971).

In practice it is also likely that decisions will be made not only
about risks as things which may go wrong but also about things
which have already gone wrong. Working with older people is
therefore about giving help with existing lacks or losses as much
as about managing risk of further loss. In reality these are, of
course, largely inseparable for the purposes of analysis and
action. A current need is a hazard to the danger of further deterioration.

ASSESSMENT

Chapter 1 was principally concerned with offering a review of
ways of 'understanding' old age and ageing. Chapter 2 was more
concerned with 'identification' and 'description' of some of the
more common hazards. Assessment is concerned with both understanding and with describing, but also with a number of other
elements, including defining, measuring, evaluating, etc. Each
of these words raises difficulties and complexities and some basic
issues in assessing older people can be identified. Emphasis has
been put on the importance of what has been called 'a total assessment' of the older person. One way of using this expression
has been to stress the importance of looking at all aspects of an
older person's behaviour, functioning and social world to gain a
'total picture'. While this is a laudable proposition, it should also
take account of several other components.

1 Assessment, as the collection of descriptive information, is
   influenced by the orientation of the person seeking the information. He will affect the description of 'the problem' by
   limiting the available definitions and he will place his own
   interpretation on the information collected.

2 The collection of information about need is meaningless unless it is related to some norm of satisfaction in the form of
practical services or other goals. Assessment should be
purposeful. The gathering of information for its own sake
serves no purpose. Making decisions should involve clear
goal setting and it is particularly important in working with
older people that goals should be realistic and achievable.

3 A 'total assessment' must take account of the will and capacity of people to define their own needs and dangers and to
influence the course of their lives. An assessment is incomplete unless it recognizes the older person's definition of
the world. This is not to suggest that his definition is in
some sense more correct but that it is at least as important
as that of anyone else. The definitions and interpretations
made by everyone involved in assessment are likely to change
during the process of interaction.

4 Good assessment depends on good communication. Useful discussions of communication with older people in the social work
context already exist (Brearley, 1975a; Gray and Isaacs,
1979; Rowlings, 1981) and are recommended.

A full assessment of risk must be conducted on several levels.
Within an area or locality it will be necessary to develop information for planning purposes by collecting data on the number and
general circumstances of all older people: this can be used to predict potential costs as demands for services on the basis of
known risk predictors (hazards). A more accurate planning measure may be developed from the categorization of eligibility for
services on current allocation assumptions and matching of categories with data on older people in that area. This again gives a
measure of potential cost in services rather than risks to older
people. The development of screening procedures takes this
over-all approach closer to identifying and measuring potential
dangers to specific older people. Unfortunately, screening methods are as yet undeveloped and unsophisticated. Assessing the
individual involves several possible approaches:

1 The problem balance sheet: listing and categorizing diseases
and other problems, as well as strengths. The latter point is
especially important: action with older people, as will be
shown later, is most successful when it builds on existing
strengths.

2 Measures of functional capacity: what tasks can be performed,
including self-care tasks, role requirements and relationship
activities.

3 Adaptation: how does the individual behave and feel about
events.

4 Identifying the match between needs and the environment /
resources to meet these needs.

In measuring risk to individuals it is necessary to identify current problems/hazards - diseases, disabilities and social hazards - in order to predict possible dangers. This must be linked to measurement of current strengths - functional abilities, existing social supports, adaptive capacities - which can be used to offset the hazards and reduce the likelihood of the feared loss or damage. This must then be related to two further assessments: assessment of the environment and assessment of potential resources. Assessing the environment may include anything from a home visit by an occupational therapist to identify and overcome practical problems of daily living (Thomas, 1978) to measuring the quality of life in a residential home. Considerable work has been done in the latter context and excellent reviews are available (Ward, 1980; Hughes and Wilkin, 1980). In assessing resources at least three factors are important: the relevance of a resource in meeting need or reducing risk, the availability of the resource, and the priority of the individual for the service. Some of these issues will be developed in the following chapters.

Finally, risk analysis involves balancing likelihood against the value of consequences: are some outcomes worth the attendant risks? Particularly important will be situations of emergency.

RECOGNIZING EMERGENCIES

Much of what has been written about emergencies in social work has been based on work on crisis theory and crisis intervention. This position is complicated by the fact that people commonly talk of crises when they are referring to emergencies but do not use the concept in the sense in which it is used in 'crisis theory'. A further complication is that the idea of emergency sometimes tends to be bound up, in the minds of doctors and social workers, with the need for compulsory action. Some hospitals, for instance, are reported to make compulsory procedures a condition of admission when an emergency occurs outside normal hours (Oram, 1978).

Although the concepts of crisis and crisis theory do have helpful ideas to offer, it is unnecessarily complicated to refer to both crisis and emergency. This is partly because crisis is a word used to mean several things, but also because it is inaccurate to assume that all crises are emergencies. The death of a close relative or a child leaving home may be crises in the sense that they create change and require new adaptations, but they do not necessarily require immediate, hurried action. In defining emergencies, then, two things seem important: first, the need to take immediate action to avoid disaster or, alternatively, the need for immediate action after serious loss or damage has occurred. An emergency is a situation in which serious danger is imminent and action must be taken to avoid loss, damage or further damage following recent loss. It would probably be more appropriate to speak of urgent situations than emergencies.

The majority of older people in the community do seem to have help available to them if an emergency should arise. A survey of people over 65 living at home (Hunt, 1978) found that 42.9 per cent of all older people felt they could ask three or four different neighbours if they needed help urgently. However, 10 per cent of the whole sample felt they would not feel able to ask anyone and this proportion rose to 12 per cent among those aged over 75 years. The bedfast and house-bound were the most likely to say they had no one to ask, but since these are the people least likely to live alone this may refer to occasions when they might be left alone. At least one in ten of all older people in this survey felt they would have no one to rely on in an emergency. Even more serious than this is the situation of some special groups. A survey in a number of London boroughs of older people in various living circumstances found that 99 per cent of people in sheltered housing, 75 per cent waiting in the community for admission to residential homes and 83 per cent of those considered suitable for sheltered housing were dependent on people outside the household for day-to-day and emergency help by virtue of the fact that they lived alone. Of those in private households, one-third said they would find it difficult to obtain help if taken ill in the middle of the night and 10 per cent of those in sheltered housing said the same. Living alone and not having access to a telephone made the difficulty of getting help in an emergency more likely (Plank, 1977). Other studies have confirmed the importance to the older person's confidence of having a telephone so that he would be able to summon help in an emergency (Gregory and Young, 1972). The telephone does not, however, seem to make much difference to general social contacts (Hunt, 1978). It is clear, then, that the more vulnerable elderly are also those most likely to be without people to rely on in an emergency.

The most common response to emergency among the elderly seems to be admission to some form of institutional care. A DHSS (1976) survey of admissions of elderly applicants for residential care suggests that a careful assessment of applicants is often not possible because many requests for admission present themselves as emergencies. In one large county it was estimated that 40 to 50 per cent of admissions were presented as emergencies. The time span of such an 'emergency' may be open to a variety of definitions. In a small study of fifty-five residents Shaw and Walton found that time spent waiting for admission ranged from two years to a few hours: the average wait was 3 months but the median wait was 3 weeks (1979). In a survey of thirty-three consecutive admissions to homes in Mid Glamorgan, Pope (1980) found that in terms of age and medical condition there was little difference between those who were admitted in haste and those who came in under other circumstances. The findings of this study have been outlined in Chapter 2 and the most important aspect seems to be the change of circumstances of those providing support for the older person which precipitates the admission. In a

small number of cases of relatively isolated people deterioration
had been slow but steady and in all but one case offers of preventive help had been made long before. For these people emergency need was the result of illness aggravated by months or
years of self-neglect. Another small group were characterized
by the need for a roof over their heads caused by unexpected
events. This finding is given some support from a small study
in Yorkshire in which two main groups of residents were identified: those who came in because they needed virtually nursing
care and a smaller number who came in because there was no
alternative residence available at the time of admission (Cigno,
1979).

The importance of precipitating factors emerges also in four
studies, quoted by Moroney (1976), which have identified similar reasons why people seek admission to care. The main reason
given is an inability or anticipated inability of the older person
to care for himself. Admission is often preceded and perhaps
precipitated by an illness or the death of a family member who
provided care. A study of admissions in Coventry concludes that
'the more subjective perception of risk is a significant discrim-
inator' and the authors draw attention to two groups of people
for whom residential homes meet a particular need.

> The first group consists of those living alone and isolated from
> friends and neighbours, for whom no change in risk is evi-
> dent and who make the application themselves, or who exper-
> ience a change in their medical condition. Often among this
> group admission follows swiftly on application. The second
> group are those living with families who experience a change
> in the pattern of family support and on whose behalf the fam-
> ily makes an application for admission (Carter and Evans, 1978,
> p. 94.

From this evidence it seems that emergencies are most likely to
arise from hazards that occur unexpectedly and for which there
has been no time to prepare. Most older people at risk are able
to wait for at least a little time. Those who cannot wait and who
constitute true emergencies - rather than panic situations - seem
most frequently to be in three broad categories:

1 Those being supported by other people following a change in
  the circumstances of the supporters.
2 Those living alone in circumstances of long-standing self-
  neglect for whom a sudden or unexpected illness may precipitate urgent need.
3 Those who have no roof over their heads: perhaps through
  fire, flood, illness of landlady, etc.

As a final point, it should be noted that, although this evidence is drawn mainly from surveys of admission to residential
care, and it has already been noted that the most commonly

sought response to emergency is institutional resources, this is not the only response. Not all older people want to go into hospital or a home and there is ample evidence that transition from house to institution brings additional risks to people who are already frail and under stress.

DECISIONS AND RISK

An important element in understanding risks is the attitudes of older people to their risks as well as the attitudes of those around them. Some attention has been given to the attitudes of society in general to the elderly at risk in the two previous chapters and some consideration must now be given to the response of older people to decision making in risky situations. There is, of course, a difference between discussing decisions made in conditions of uncertainty and decisions made about clearly identifiable hazards and dangers. Being old, for instance, is risky in that it introduces potential costs and dangers but the attitude to 'being old' is likely to be of a different order from attitudes to climbing stairs, giving up a home or other concrete hazards. Decisions about specific hazards will be made against the general complexity of a range of factors which contribute to attitudes to the uncertainties of old age.

For a general discussion of research and attitudes to risk reference should be made to the introductory book in this series (Brearley, 1982). Four particularly important elements can be summarized:

1 Risks may be misestimated for a number of subjective and psychologically determined reasons.
2 Risks may not be seen as such and therefore ignored.
3 Risks may be seen in terms of levels of acceptability. This may point towards the possibility of developing a hierarchy of acceptability.
4 The prior set, or the world view of the individual will also affect perception of the risk.

Some of these points can be picked up and developed in relation to older people although there is relatively little supporting evidence. Little research work has been done specifically about attitudes of older people on the risk dimension. One obvious speculative point is that if the world view of the observer or actor is important to decision making under risk, and we know that older people tend to have low expectations, then it might be logical to assume that older people will expect low gains and be less willing to take risks.

In early research it was found that the older person generally needed a larger probability of success than a younger person (Wallach and Kogan, 1961) and that the attitude change in ageing was more abrupt for men than for women. Botwinick (1966) provided supporting evidence in a study which suggested that older people were less willing to advise a risky course of action than were younger ones. Several years later, however, the same author found that when some risk was unavoidable old and young were comparably cautious (Botwinick, 1969). More recent research comparing a group of undergraduates and a group in the age range 55 to 65 using the choice-dilemma questionnaire found that the groups did not differ on initial decisions or after discussion in groups (Spence et al., 1974). Okun and Siegler (1976) showed that older adults given a choice between more or less difficult vocabulary tests chose the easier ones: older people were seen as more cautious. Later findings (Okun and Elias, 1977) suggest that where the size of pay offs is contingent on the size of the risk older people were not more cautious than younger adults. It appears, then, from laboratory-based psychological research that older adults select lower risk alternatives when there is no incentive to do otherwise.

Some research has been conducted in more specific contexts. A study of addiction to drug-taking among older people in the United States found that their perceptions of the risk involved partly explained attitudes. Older respondents appeared to perceive more over all risk and the financial risk appeared to contribute most to decision making (Beardon et al., 1979). In research into responses to natural disasters early work assumed that the elderly would over-report their problems and express feelings of relative deprivation (Friedsam, 1962). More recent research offers varying conclusions. A study following the collapse of the Teton Dam in Idaho found that older people coped quite well with disaster and tended to report fewer adverse emotional effects and feelings of relative deprivation than younger victims (Huerta and Horton, 1978). Similarly a study of tornado victims in Nebraska suggested that the coping capacity of older people actually surpasses that of younger victims who experienced more changes, higher anxiety and physical stress levels, regardless of the damage suffered (Bell, 1978).

The evidence about attitudes to risk among the elderly is complex and much of it is very preliminary. There is some reason to believe that there are age-related differences but, as with much of such research, it is not clear how far this is due to age changes and how far to different life experiences between age groups. Older people may, however, be more cautious unless there is good reason not to be so.

Some attempts to develop models of the decision-making process among older people have emerged. A preliminary distinction should be made between decisions which are prompted by major life events and which are therefore primarily about the relative merits, cost, gains and risks of significant life changes and those decisions which are made more by default. Some decisions are not so much about change but about maintenance of the status quo and it must be stressed that often success in work with older people is marked not by change but by no-change: maintenance

of a situation is a gain over time if the alternative was deterioration. Guttman (1978) proposes a four-stage model of decision
making among the elderly. Stage one involves an awareness of a
need or problem; stage two engages the individual in seeking a
solution, alternatives are created and relative costs, utilities, or
values are weighed; in stage three a selection is made and decisions taken about whether or not to act; and in stage four the
action is evaluated. Similar models have been developed by others
in extended and more complex form (Beaver, 1979).

The stress in this model is on decision making as a rational
process and there is little, if any, evidence that the majority of
older people are able to make decisions in such a clear-cut way.
Constraints on decision making through limitations on choice and
access to information have already been discussed. In one study
of older people in residential care it was found that of fifty-five
residents only eight had been given information before admission,
a further eleven had received reassurance and only two had been
given any warning about the experience (Shaw and Walton, 1979).
One way of helping to improve the possibility of rational and careful decision making will be to improve communication and therefore the quality of information.

RESOURCES AND NEEDS

It would be unreasonable to proceed to discuss the use of resources in an operational situation without giving some thought
to the over all development and deployment of those resources.
Consideration was given earlier to some of the assumptions which
underlie provision for older people. Mention has been made of
the objectives of policy outlined in 'A Happier Old Age', the government discussion document (DHSS, 1978), which stressed the
need to ensure that retirement does not mean poverty, and identified the importance of enabling older people to enjoy choice
and to remain independent in their own homes for as long as possible.

It should also be emphasized again that discussions of helping
services can too easily fall into the trap of discussing older
people as if they all had problems with which they require the
help of services. This is not so. The majority of old people do
live in their own homes, are not in poverty, alone or lonely.
Most older people are not ill, disabled or dependent on others
and the vast majority are living in their own homes and providing and receiving help in interaction with family and friends.
The discussion of policies to meet the needs of the elderly should
therefore be concerned with two dimensions. First, policies
should ensure a minimum quality of life through the maintenance
of basic resources, as of right, to all older people: sufficient
provision to enjoy not merely a level of survival but also a degree of active enjoyment - leisure and pleasure. Second, it will
be necessary to ensure minimum standards for certain statutory

provisions to meet the needs of those who do find old age a time of problems. There are, as has been shown earlier, a number of prevalent assumptions about the position and role of older people and these are matched by assumptions about the effect and purpose of services. Assumptions are made, for instance, about the role and responsibilities of the family to provide care, on the one hand, and about the willingness or reluctance of families to take on such responsibilities, on the other hand. Similarly, there are assumptions about services, about the relationship of formal and informal services, and about older people's attitudes to and demand for such services. Many of these assumptions are general in nature and largely unfounded in fact and much research must be undertaken before we have a clear picture.

In considering the over all social provision for older people in the community, three broad issues are of importance. Some problems relate to the resources of older people, which are likely to be lower than the resources of those who have access to work: older people rely mainly on pensions derived from the state, with a smaller group dependent on private pensions and income from investments. Second, issues arise relating to the living conditions of older people, particularly their housing, health and social interactions. Third, there are a number of problems of 'formulating and especially implementing the various sectorial policies so that services and programmes can be consistently organized by taking account of geographical and socio-economic disparities and involving the elderly themselves from an active retirement standpoint' (Organization for Economic Co-operation and Development, 1979, p. 155). It is not possible here to develop these questions but a general point can be made about two approaches to policy development.

There is a difference between the view of resources which stresses the economic costs and an alternative view which stresses the social costs. In Chapter 1 reference was made to the difference between the organizational perspective and the humanitarian perspective on policy and provision for older people and this distinction relates very closely to the division between the 'economic' and 'social-need' views. In the former view the emphasis on decision making about provisions will be on the costs to the community of provision. In the social-need view emphasis is much more likely to be on assessing the individual's situation and to measuring the costs to that individual.

This distinction moves the discussion towards a focus on the provision of services to meet individual needs. Before proceeding with this, attention should be drawn to an important question asked by Johnson: 'Do we really need social services for older people?' (1979). He poses the question primarily as a challenge to the assumption that increasing numbers of older people will mean increasing demand for social services and makes the particularly important point that for the immediate future greater numbers does not mean greater demand: 'To put it more correctly it will merely mean more unmet need.' Older people have low ex-

pectations of welfare provisions and tend not to ask for help and
the level of provision is likely to increase more slowly than will
the number of older people. The consequence is likely to be that
social services will be more and more a provision for very old
and dependent people: more a provision of 'maintenance at minimum cost' (Brearley, 1980).

Related to the distinction between economic and social need
perspectives, there has been considerable discussion of the importance of maintaining a balance between 'cash and care' in
providing for older people. 'A Happier Old Age' (DHSS, 1978)
pointed out that public expenditure on cash benefits is much
greater than on services and asked whether this balance should
be changed. Put in this form the question is over-simplified and
few of the published responses took up the question. The Personal Social Services Council (1978) argued that the question
was clearly unrealistic at a time when over one-third of all retired people are living at or near the poverty line. The Disability
Alliance (1979) pointed out that the problem is not so much choosing between cash and care as identifying those categories of
older people who are in need of both. They argue that severely
disabled older people are urgently in need of both cash and services. The balance is clearly a very complex one and a simple
cash or care contrast does not reveal the full dimensions. To
take a simple example: extra income will not buy non-existent
services for a 94-year-old, yet, on the other hand, research on
increasing the home-help service has shown a disappointing take
up because some who might have benefited could not afford the
service (Ham and Smith, 1978).

Both the economic and social-need views will be concerned in
different ways with matching service to need. This will involve
at least three issues for policy. First, developing services depends on an awareness of cost-effectiveness. A major preoccupation, for example, has been with the relative costs and benefits of residential care in comparison to other forms of substitute
or additional services. Second, policy development depends on
identifying ways of allocating priorities: of deciding which needs
are to receive which services and distributing resources according to an agreed and rational basis. Third, it is necessary to
develop a form of organization of services which will deliver help
appropriately (both effectively and sensitively).

One issue which is of major importance is developing ways of
working with older people. Much service delivery is concerned
with providing things for, or around, older people, or with doing
things to, or on behalf of, them. It seems important to explore
approaches to working with older people in the future. This has
a number of justifications: partly in terms of the benefits to the
individual of being involved and therefore maintaining or re-
learning skills, partly because individuals play a central part in
defining their needs and influencing their circumstances and
partly as a value statement - they have a right to be involved.
There are two dimensions to this: individual plans should be

worked out with each older person and area or community planning should be done with the older people of the area.

It has been argued that

it is doubtful that one could find a large community anywhere
that has a completely satisfactorily balanced and coordinated
program for the elderly. This means that there is a need for
planning with and for the elderly, to meet the problems of
aging. There should be planning by the national government
in conjunction with non-governmental organizations if they
exist. But planning must also be done in local communities,
because that is where people live (Dunham et al., 1978, p. 3).

There have been varying arguments about the respective roles
of local and central government in planning for ageing. Some
writers have stessed the role of central government in setting
broad lines of policy for local authorities (Taylor, 1979). Others
have outlined the problems attendant on developing a local social-
policy programme for older people (Smith, 1979). The most obvious problems are the range of agencies involved and the complexities of the relationships between them. Another problem is
the demands made by central government for joint planning at
local level but the lack of any corresponding corporate or co-
operative co-ordination of central government planning. Not only
are there problems of joint planning but also problems relating to
the day-to-day operation of a system of caring resources with
rigid administrative boundaries.

Developing social services for older people should be done in
the recognition that the majority of older people do not make
demands on specialist services. The use of social services in an
operational context to meet need or to manage risk must recognize both the individual needs and the organizational and economic imperatives. There are limited resources and potentially
almost unlimited needs and matching of needs and services is
therefore a complex task.

BUILDING ON THE STRENGTHS

Three basic aims of service delivery can be highlighted: alleviation, enrichment and prevention (Baltes, 1973). Although originally proposed in the context of psychological intervention,
these would seem to be goals of equal relevance to any form of
service. It is important to alleviate the problems experienced by
older people but far more desirable to be able to prevent difficulties or to reduce risk and even more attractive to think in
terms of improving and enriching their lives. Sadly, much of
the involvement of helping professionals is concerned with re-
solving difficulties after they have occurred: with alleviation. A
slightly different perspective on these goals, stressing the importance of risk management, will emphasize the reduction of

hazards or deficiencies and the building of strengths to offset
the effects of hazards and therefore to reduce the likelihood of
loss or damage.

The need to build on existing strengths is important but relatively little attention has been given to this aspect of involvement with older people. Much more emphasis is usually put on
coping with loss and compensating for deficits. Blunden and
Kushlick (1974) have identified three types of strengths among
older people. First, there are the strengths of older people themselves: even the most profoundly disabled or mentally infirm
person has some abilities available to him. Second, there are the
strengths represented by the people available to deliver services: these may be professional or voluntary helpers, or family
and friends. Third, there are the procedures which are available
for helping. These procedures fall into four groups, which are
not mutually exclusive: the procedures of medicine or surgery;
the procedures of teaching or rehabilitation; the provision of a
prosthetic environment, including both physical and social pros-
theses; and restrictive procedures, which must be used in a
limited and well-monitored way. The authors argue that these
strengths can be used and extended through what they term
'engagement'. A person is said to be engaged in his environment
if he is interacting with people or things in a way which is likely
to develop or maintain skills and abilities.

The concept of engagement is a useful one but this approach
is by no means the only way to develop strengths. The strengths
can be summarized briefly as the skills and abilities (including
the beliefs, attitudes and will) of the older person; the skills and
abilities of others available to help; and the procedures and environments which are available. The rest of this book will be concerned to elaborate on ways of developing these strengths.

USING PRACTICAL RESOURCES

From any discussion of the use of social services' resources a
dilemma emerges. There is a wish to provide older people with
access to a range of services which are, first, alternatives in
the sense that they realistically offer equivalent levels of care
and which are, second, different from each other, in order to
provide for the fact that different people will want to live their
lives in different ways. In conflict with this is the importance of
ensuring a fair and equitable distribution of scarce resources
among a large group of people with needs to be met.

It is clear from an examination of the use and allocation of domiciliary services that methods of assessments of individual need
are inadequate and that services are patchily spread throughout
the country, so that people in some areas receive a higher level
of service, although their level of incapacity may be no lower. It
is also clear that the generally presented picture of community
care as an alternative to residential care is too simplistically

drawn. Residential care provides a level of personal care which
is rarely available to the older person in the community. At the
same time it may also offer positive benefits and the term 'residential care' is a blanket term which itself includes a very wide
range of different resources. Community care commonly represents an unco-ordinated set of different facilities separately
administered and frequently run without reference to a co-
operative plan. In consequence many older people are unable to
move within and between facilities. At the same time it must be
recognised that the level of provision in the community is not up
to the tasks expected of it and provision is increasingly for the
very old, frail and dependent.

Within the context of existing formal services the answer to
the question, 'What can be done with services?', can be a depressing one. All that can be done for many older people is to
provide stop-gap solutions offering a minimal level of care and
protection. The over-all picture is not, however, entirely one of
gloom and progress is being made in three broad directions.
First, a number of innovative schemes are being developed
throughout the country; second, several approaches to developing more flexible forms and packages of resources have been
established; and, third, there is a growing recognition of the
importance of informal supports in the care of old people. Some
of the issues can be outlined:

1 Innovations

A preliminary question must be to ask whether innovations are
necessarily desirable and why they arise. A simple answer may
be that it is unreasonable to expect existing resources to expand
without limit. It has already been established here that 'need' in
the context of provision is defined normatively: the level of need
is measured in terms of criteria at any point in time for a specific service. There must come a point at which the interaction of
felt need - what people want - with what others are prepared to
provide reaches a no-growth level. In such circumstances, progress towards meeting expressed needs with limited resources
can only be made by a more imaginative use of what already exists or by developing entirely new approaches to meeting particular needs. Another reason which may account for innovation may
be impatience with existing services and with the pace of change
in organizations. Innovations may arise from a creative and imaginative drive to provide a better service but they may also grow
from the frustrations caused by inadequate provision. In either
event one danger is that innovations will be inadequately evaluated and controlled. A further danger is that they be seen as
providing a better service in the sense of an economically less
costly provision. This is only a danger if this is at the expense
of less immediately obvious but equally valuable benefits.

Innovations in services for the elderly are too numerous to
classify or list in detail here. Some valuable lists are available
and can be strongly recommended. Some of the more commonly

quoted experiments, ranging from the Oxford fish scheme (emergency display cards for vulnerable older people) to a universal daughter scheme in Hastings (befriending of the lonely), are
listed by Gray and Isaacs (1979). A compendium of schemes is
provided by the Association of County Councils (1979). This
lists such domiciliary and community activities as relief care in
private households in Buckinghamshire, an evening care scheme
in Essex, a residential home-help scheme in Gloucestershire, etc.
Schemes involving innovations in accommodation and developments
in Health and Social Services co-operation are also noted. Joint
schemes involving co-operative ventures run by statutory and
voluntary services include a club run in a school in Clwyd for
the local elderly, local street-link schemes, and the involvement
of school children in a 'hypothermia' project in East Sussex. A
catalogue of developments in care is also provided by the Personal Social Services Council (1980). This draws mainly from a
survey of local authorities and identifies, particularly, innovations in care of mentally infirm older people, in the provision
of care for older people for whom residential or hospital care
might once have seemed inevitable, and schemes encouraging the
involvement of older people in the running of services. An additional directory of innovations has also been provided by the Kent
University Personal Social Services Research Unit (Ferlie, 1980).

From this evidence it is abundantly clear that there are large
numbers of existing developments in many areas of care for
older people. Some of these are aimed at the development of a
more flexible use of existing services. The development of the
home-help service in Coventry, for instance, shows that although
additional funds and extended provision are important they are
no more important than

> the changing philosophy of service with its emphasis on a
> broader range of care - the increased flexibility of hours and
> visits, the changing role of home helps and organisers, the
> use of specialist workers, and the increased training and sup-
> port of home helps (Latto, 1980, p. 21).

Other approaches have set out to fill conspicuous gaps in existing services. The problems experienced by older people following discharge home from hospital, for instance, have been
well recognized (Age Concern, Greater London, 1980; Skeet,
1970). The Continuing Care Project was established to encourage
the development of after-care arrangements for older patients
following discharge from hospital and recommends the development of local co-ordination policies to plan for such arrangements
(Continuing Care Project, 1980). Similarly other projects have
attempted to build on long-recognized approaches. Boarding-out
schemes or lodgings schemes have been established for many
years (National Old People's Welfare Council, 1969), but until
recently have had little conspicuous success. During the late
1970s a number of schemes apparently achieved more success

within the changing context of provision (Newton, 1980; Leeds
City Council, 1979; Barley and Wilson, 1979).

The main contribution of innovations in services seems to be
in the recognition of the need to use resources flexibly. Different areas and individuals all have needs which require a range
of alternative approaches.

2 Flexible care

It has been established that there is a degree of shortfall in the
provision of services to older people. The extent of this shortfall is difficult to measure for at least two reasons. First, the
lack of clear statements of welfare goals makes it impossible to
do more than make general statements about apparent deficiencies in relation to current usage of resources. Second, there is
little information about the relative effectiveness of different
forms of intervention with older people experiencing different
forms of welfare shortfalls (Bebbington, 1978). In a study of
over 500 people over retirement age, Chapman (1979) reported
unmet needs for help which was available from health, welfare
and financial services and benefits in almost half the respondents. Following referral of almost all these needs to relevant
services it was still found, six months later, that only 43 per
cent of the 379 items of practical help had actually been received.
Reasons for this included failure by the relevant services to provide help (due, to a large extent, to the failure of one voluntary
agency because of heavy demand for its services); ineligibility
of the older people to receive help; time-lags between processes
of assessment and provision which led to needs being overtaken
by events (death, hospital admission, help from relatives, etc.);
the majority (42 per cent) were not received either because of
refusal to accept help or because of failure to complete applications. Reasons for the rejection of help were given as the feeling that need was not sufficiently great, or a wish to be self-
reliant or dissatisfaction with what was offered. Chapman
concludes that there are two forms of need. The first, which he
calls negative need, is not available to be met unless there are
quantitative and qualitative improvements in services. The second, positive need, can be met, if better ways of identifying
need are available.

In considering approaches to more imaginative uses of resources,
two fundamental issues are therefore important. The predominant
response to presented need among the elderly is either to seek
admission to residential care or to allocate a limited amount of
domiciliary services to a relatively small number of highly dependent and 'at risk' older people. In addition there is a considerable amount of unmet need for practical help, not only among
those who might be regarded as being on the borderline of eligibility for service but also amongst those with a high degree of
dependency (Plank, 1977; Chapman, 1979). From these perspectives three elements of the need for flexibility in future developments seem important:

1 a more imaginative use of resources to meet existing need.
2 differential use of resources to increase their acceptability
to those who reject help in its present form.
3 better information and identification procedures to recognize
unmet need and to ensure that older people are aware of entitlement to resources.

In order to begin to meet some of these requirements it has to
be recognized that change needs to take place on many levels.
The planning and co-ordination of services within an area or
locality are essential to provide a caring system within which individual packages of care can be developed. At an individual
level all professional and voluntary workers can contribute to
meeting both individual and family need by a flexible use of resources. If these practical supports can be used imaginatively,
they can be directed towards the objectives of maximum integration and safety for the older person. Some important innovations have begun to translate these possibilities into reality.
One of the most widely quoted and reported schemes is the
'Community Care Project' developed by Kent Social Services
Department and the Personal Social Services Unit at the University of Kent (Challis and Davies, 1980). The aims of the scheme
have been summarized as including

the improvement of services to elderly clients by providing
more flexible, individually tailored services in conjunction with
those currently available and the more effective utilisation of
resources by either the postponement or reduction of the need
for residential care.

The mechanism to achieve these aims was 'the provision of a de-
centralized budget to experienced social workers who would take
responsibility for the coordination and development of care for
the elderly people' (p. 5). The outline guidelines for the project
were that clients would be those who would otherwise be eligible
for admission to residential care; a weekly limit on expenditure
on each client was fixed at two-thirds of the marginal cost of a
place in residential home; and the unit cost of existing depart-
mental services was included in making decisions about costs per
client. The authors of the report make the important point that
a balance has to be found between the organizational need for
procedures which ensure accountability and the freedom for a
more flexible response. This is a key factor in the development
of any flexibility of service use. A preliminary evaluation of this
scheme notes that fewer clients in the experimental group entered
residential care and that the scheme was beneficial to the client
by most of the criteria used. Although some evidence is given to
suggest that this is provided at lower cost than would otherwise
have been involved, this is a complex calculation: some relative
cost advantage seems, however, to exist.
This was the first major project of its kind in the United King-

dom and some replications have since been established. It seems
to point towards the desirability of a more flexible approach, involving a wide range of services. The important principle is to
begin with the needs expressed and perceived in the situation of
the older person and to seek appropriate resources from both
informal and formal sources to meet these needs. Many of the difficulties experienced by older people are the result of an over
rigid definition of eligibility for services which have been com-
partmentalized. It should not be necessary for an older person
to convert his need into terms acceptable to agencies. Needs are
not 'for a home help', or 'for residential resources': in the first
instance they are felt in much more general terms and a flexible
service will fit the services to the client, not vice versa.

3 Informal care

An increasing recognition of the importance of informal support
in the maintenance of older people in the community has led to
discussion of the balance between state and family care. The
great preponderance of help for older people is provided from
informal sources - family, friends and neighbours (Plank, 1979).
However, there has been a marked decline in the availability of
family to provide support in recent years (Moroney, 1976). In
part this is a consequence of changes in the proportion of people
with traditional caring roles in the community. More women, for
instance, are in employment (although changes in patterns of
unemployment may affect this situation) and there are relatively
fewer single women. More importantly the increasing proportion
of very old people has meant that many more older people do not
have anyone available to provide support. As was pointed out
earlier, over one-third of people over the age of 75 are likely to
be without any living offspring and 45 per cent of older people
living alone, but with surviving children, would like to see them
more often than they actually do (Abrams, 1978). Where children
do live nearby, however, older parents can generally expect to
receive a significant amount of help and support. The role of
friends and neighbours is as important as that of the family and
even more so for some older people. Only one older person in
fifty neither receives nor makes any visits to either friends or
family (Hunt, 1978).

There are at least two distinct issues, therefore. A substantial
minority of older people have few social contacts and therefore
lack the help and support of other people. Second, it has been
argued that the role of the family in providing care has become
less significant.

To develop the latter point, it has been proposed that the increase in state provision has undermined the responsibility of the
family to provide care. However, it is just as much of an over-
simplification to argue that official action weakens family support
as it would be to suggest that a caring and supportive family will
obviate the need for any formal or official action. A very different perspective on the same issue proposes that formal services

tend to emphasize the moral duty of families to care. Stressing
the point, to stimulate discussion, an Age Concern document
argues that what is needed is

> a recognition that the nuclear family cannot be extended to in-
> clude the old.... The burden of responsibility lies not with
> families (who may, for many years, have had only fleeting con-
> tact with their older relatives) but with the older relatives'
> own social groupings.... Too often voluntary helpers castigate
> families for selfishly ignoring the needs of their ageing rel-
> atives, not realizing that it is now the voluntary helper's
> responsibility, as part of the old person's social network,
> themselves, to take on those tasks (Bowder, 1980, p. 7).

Whether or not families have a moral responsibility to care,
those older people who do have relatives are generally given,
and give in return, help and support: people accept a mutual
responsibility. The more important issue is the relationship between official and informal support. In practice, social services
are used to give support to the supporters in relatively few
ways. It has been shown earlier that domiciliary services are
overwhelmingly provided for older people living alone or with
only an elderly spouse. Residential resources are used predominantly to care for isolated and frail older people. Some
efforts have been made to support families through extending
the opportunity for short-term care in residential homes to give
families some respite, and through intermittent care in hospitals.
Similarly day-care and day-hospital facilities have been increasingly provided and these give relief to relatives in sharing the
care of older people (Brocklehurst, 1978; Morley, 1979).

From the point of view of formal services the dilemma remains,
however. In order to release resources to provide help for families to prevent breakdown, it would be necessary to reduce the
provision to those isolated and very old people who are less
likely to have informal supports. Since, statistically, family
breakdown represents a relatively small demand on those formal
services which are allocated in meeting individual need, it seems
unlikely that a major shift in state resources to 'supporting the
supporters' will take place.

What is certain is that the role of informal networks and supports in provision for the older population requires more detailed
and careful analysis. Some very useful preliminary work has been
done (see, for example, Abrams, P., 1977), but our understanding of some of the basic elements of community support is very
limited. Put at its simplest: what does support mean? This seems
to include concepts of practical services, friendly visiting, neigh-
bourly companionship, contact, lifelines, etc., none of which has
yet been adequately defined.

Particularly important to the concept of community care in the
United Kingdom is the role of volunteers. On one level, there are
a number of important issues about the over-all place of volun-

teers in the caring system. As Clarke has asked: 'Who has identified the matters of principle which should be applied in determining the part to be played by volunteers within the social
policies for the coming decade?' (1980, p. 19). On a different
level, there is now a considerable amount of information about
the role and use of volunteers in day-to-day practical situations
(see, for example, Darvill, 1980; Harbridge, 1980a).

A further point of importance here is that discussions of
informal networks and older people stress their position as
recipients. This is an over-simplification in a number of ways.
Relationships are reciprocal and older people do perform valuable
services for others in many ways - not least of which is the
grandparental role. The development of politically active and
aware groups among older people, particularly in the London
area, has been an important feature of the 1970s and this is
likely to become an increasingly important component in the future. A number of reports of the development of community groups
involving older people in helping themselves are particularly significant (Glendenning (ed.), 1978; Buckingham et al., 1979) and
Oriol's discussion of political advocacy in the USA also points to
important potential changes (1981).

MAINTAINING AND PROTECTING

It has not been the purpose of this chapter to give a detailed
description and classification of the resources that are available
to help older people. The objective has been to raise some of the
main issues that are current in attempts to find ways of using
resources creatively.

Underlying the discussion are two fundamental issues for the
distribution of resources:

1 The practical day-to-day business of providing services
   depends on the maintenance of a precarious balance between
   the needs of individual older people and the scarcity of resources. One consequence is that, viewed in terms of equity,
   many older people have a 'fair' share of available resources,
   in the sense that they have as much as others in comparable
   situations, but they also bear an unacceptable burden of
   risk. In other words, current levels and usage of resources
   are insufficient to remove risk and need.
2 The need to use resources flexibly and imaginatively must be
   balanced with the demands of organizations and society that
   workers should be accountable for their use of these resources. Accountability is an important element in the maintenance of the balance outlined in point 1 above.

In addition, in the actual allocation of resources, two central
points are paramount:

3 In the allocation of resources the means of assessment and
the criteria of allocation are frequently unclear. These must
be priority areas for development and the framework for
risk analysis and management provides some basis for progress.
4 In creating packages of care for older individuals it is important to build on existing strengths and to recognize the
capacity - and the right - of the individual to take an active
part in deciding and in acting on his own behalf.

Finally, it should be noted that although the terms need/'in
need' and risk/'at risk' have been used largely interchangeably
in this chapter there is a difference. Need refers to a perceived
deficiency in relation to a goal of satisfaction and if the need is
met the older person can continue to function. Risk refers to a
future possibility and the reduction of risk is therefore necessary to prevention. However, a person 'in need' is also, by definition, 'at risk', in so far as need creates the possibility of
danger. The terms are therefore closely linked. This is much
more than a semantic point: I have argued elsewhere (Brearley,
1975a) that care for older people fails when it deals with continuing problems by the application of static solutions. Solutions
should aim to deal not just with a limited view of needs in the
here-and-now, but should also be concerned with restoring a
normal, on-going process of growing old with the satisfaction
which that will imply. It is not enough simply to meet need and
to maintain older people, it is also important to recognize the
risks (implying both loss and gain possibilities for the future)
and to protect and, above all, to provide scope for change and
progress.

Most important of all is to find the right balance of care for
each individual between formal and informal provision and to
protect his interests and rights within a complex and often dis-
jointed and unco-ordinated set of provisions. This can only be
done in the recognition of the strengths which the older person
brings to the situation.

It should also be remembered that the safest course of action
may not necessarily be the best course of action. If being safe
means giving up self-determination and the right to choose, then
it may not be acceptable. But this, too, is a simplistic position:
the older person's decision to take risks is partly subject to the
wishes of those around him to see that he is safe. In reality,
safety judgments are made on the basis of a complex balance of
competing possibilities.

Finally, before proceeding to the subsequent chapters, reference must again be made to the importance of involving a group
of different workers in the care of older people. The importance
of establishing a multidimensional approach to older people and
their risks has been well-established. Only if clear communication between professionals is possible can a full assessment be
made, and only if such an assessment is made can the most

appropriate help be given to the older person. In one view the assessment team may be the primary-care team including general practitioner, community nurse, health visitor, home-help organizer and social worker, or the team may include the hospital group of physicians, nurses, social workers, physiotherapists and occupational therapists. Ideally, the team should include all of these although in practice various groupings exist based on organizational barriers, administrative necessities or personalities.

The literature on teamwork stresses the advantage of working together but there are considerable problems. In a discussion of social worker attachments to general medical practice, Brooks (1977) points out that potential demand for social services is virtually unlimited but requests for help from the GP take their place in the local authority scale of priorities and this offers scope for potential dispute. Brooks also identifies differences in training and differences in professional responsibility and accountability as potential sources of difficulty. Ratoff et al. (1974) suggest that doctors tend to engage in rapid decision making whereas social workers often need to proceed much more slowly and they argue that the 'impatience generated on both sides ... is a significant factor in the alienation of the two professions.' Discussing multidisciplinary meetings in a psychogeriatric unit, Jones (1980) argues that social workers can be in an uncomfortable middle position in situations of conflict between the social services' department and the medical staff over discharge of a patient. Describing care for older people in institutional situations, Wilkin and Jolley (1979) suggest yet another factor, which inhibits the development of greater collaboration between agencies, is the large populations served and the correspondingly large and complex organizations needed to provide services.

The advantages of working together are undoubted and some advanced projects have been developed (Camden, London Borough, 1978 and 1979), but a lot of careful work has to be done to develop a team awareness and mutual respect and co-operation. Teams can be cumbersome, they may be distracted from the task by interprofessional rivalries and they can be dominated by the medical members (Rowlings, 1978). One difficulty particularly noted by Rowlings is

> the lack of clarity about who is responsible for defining an acceptable degree of risk, who is responsible for protecting the frail elderly ... and who has the right of intervention .... There are perhaps useful points to be learnt from the management of child abuse cases, where the multi-disciplinary team that comes together for a case conference on a particular child or family ... is also required to make an assessment of risk and to define the role of each worker who is involved (p. 69).

A further point can be added about group assessments of the

elderly. In a discussion of the allocation procedures of places in residential homes in Coventry, Carter and Evans showed that it was not possible to know from week to week what the criteria for admission would be since resources and needs fluctuate. 'In consequence there is a tendency on the part of those supporting an application to advocate the applicant's cause, stressing a partisan view' (1978, p. 93). Case conferences, teams and other groups discussing the needs of older people are likely to be involved in negotiation: advocacy and conserving resources may be influential in reaching a definition of need and risk as much as any 'objective' data.

4 RISK AND SOCIAL WORK

Stewart Pritchard and Paul Brearley

There is little doubt that older people are in general an unpopular group in the eyes of social workers. This was made clear in Chapter 1 and is amply illustrated by an extensive survey of local authority social services' departments. (Stevenson and Parsloe et al., 1978). This survey shows that a great deal of work with older people is carried out by social-work assistants rather than by qualified workers. There is, as Rowlings has pointed out, no evidence that this is appropriate:

> neither the literature on the needs and experiences of older people, nor the case examples furnished by social services' department staff offer any evidence that in terms of client vulnerability and of case complexity the elderly are, *a priori*, a client group particularly appropriate for unqualified or ancillary workers (1978, p. 1).

In a study of a Social Services' department area team in Southampton it was found that nearly one-third of problems presented to the team were associated with physical disability, illness or ageing. This was the largest group of referrals and 84 per cent received some form of practical help (Goldberg et al., 1977). The authors commented that the service packages which these clients received reflected their needs for a range of practical support. They also concluded (with some reservations about the method of assessment) that the aims were achieved in half the cases: almost twice as high an achievement rate as in other problem categories. The work being done in these cases was mainly aimed at bringing about 'small changes in the personal/social environment by providing a service or practical aid' (p. 275).

A central debate in social work which is particularly highlighted in work with older clients is the relationship between personal counselling and service delivery. The answer to the question, 'What do social workers do with older clients?', is that they are primarily offering packages of practical services to the satisfaction of most clients (Neill et al., 1973). The answer to the question, 'Does what social workers do have any effect?', is much more complex. The only substantial study of the effectiveness of social work with this client group was conducted before the formation of social services' departments (Goldberg et al., 1970). This study found that trained social workers did not bring any more change in the physical circumstances of older clients than a group of untrained workers but they did create a generally greater improvement of morale in relation to attitudes and feelings about those physical circumstances.

The needs, deficiencies and hazards experienced by older people are predominantly material and many solutions do lie in the provision of practical aid and support in a courteous, efficient and tactful manner. There is, however, no reason to believe that older clients are any more or less likely to need help with emotional needs than other groups. There is evidence to suggest that counselling and supportive relationships used by social workers can help in certain kinds of situations. This is most conspicuously so where difficulties involving older people are related to bereavement, grief and depression, family and individual stress and decision making about, for instance, accommodation change.

Social work with older people therefore involves the efficient and flexible delivery of practical resources, both formal and informal, as well as help in situations where there are emotional and personal difficulties. Plank (1979) has argued that a flexible care system for individual older people can be co-ordinated through what he terms a case manager who would be a qualified social worker. The case manager would be responsible for thorough assessment; for constructing service packages tailored to meet individual and family needs; for counselling those who are admitted to residential care; and for counselling those who remain in the community. Although the terminology is elaborate, the key points should be stressed: co-ordination of varied services, flexibility, detailed and thorough assessment and balancing practical resources with relationship needs are essential components of social work with older people.

Two general assumptions will be made in this chapter. First, it is now well established that a wide range of skills and approaches to social work is as necessary and appropriate to older people as to other groups. Second, it is assumed here that social work intervention should be directly related to specified objectives, agreed jointly by client and social worker. The importance of clarity of objectives in creating change in the lives of older people cannot be too strongly emphasized (Brearley, 1978). Before proceeding to discuss detailed approaches, some general principles and objectives of work with older people can be outlined.

1 Independence, dependence, and interdependence: independence has been recognized as a desirable objective in work with older people for many years, yet there have been few clear attempts to specify what this means in practice. The case of Mr C, given in the Introduction, is an example of the deficiencies of the concept: his independence of services has led to an acute situation of distress and neglect and his independence of mind was leading to a perpetuation of his own unhappiness and discomfort. Independence must therefore mean something more than freedom from physical de-

pendence on others and more than a determination to be self-reliant in the face of incapacity for self-care. What seems to be particularly important is the quality of interdependence between people and the guiding principle for practice is the need to maintain a balance between independence and interdependence. This involves recognizing the need of the older person to remain a separate, respected and self-respecting individual while providing for the fact that some people need a good deal of practical and emotional support. A concern to preserve independence should also not blind us to the right of older people to be interdependent – to interact and be involved with others.

2 Knowledge and understanding: it is important to understand the meanings of experiences from the point of view of everyone involved. To take a simple example, the loss of a spouse will be distressing for anyone but the nature of the grief will be very different if the death follows a long, painful illness than if it comes suddenly at a relatively early age. It is not enough to know about objective facts but necessary also to understand subjective responses.

3 Choice and responsibility: it was agreed earlier that it is important to increase the available range of options to create more choice for older people but also recognized that such choice rarely exists. A guiding principle for action is to increase choice in the light of two broad objectives: first, choice is essential to self-determination and therefore to ensuring that people can choose the kind of old age they want; and, second, choice contributes to other desirable objectives, such as independence. It must also be recognized that the right of older people to choose is often dependent on the willingness of others to continue to provide care and support. The right to choice must be exercised responsibly.

4 Safety and freedom: there is often a conflict between the wish to maintain physical safety and enabling self-determination. Families may need support in taking the risk of not preventing the older person from taking a risk and social workers are also often realistically anxious to protect themselves from blame and guilt. A further dimension of this is the explicit recognition that some people have to be protected against themselves. Perhaps the major dimension in work with older people is concerned with seeking and maintaining the balance between safety and freedom, and protection and control.

5 Loss and transition: two perspectives which have been explored earlier are particularly important. On the one hand, old age has been described as a time when people are exposed to a greater likelihood of loss. On the other hand, it is possible to view ageing as a process of growth and development through time which will bring both losses and gains. In each of these views there is potential stress for the ageing person in the form of physical and environmental loss and hazards, and as emotional responses to loss and change.

Approaches to helping will therefore need to be concerned both with practical resources and with the provision of supportive relationships between the social worker and the older person, as well as with the development of new supporting networks within the family and community to offset hazards and to maintain strengths.

Older people most frequently come into contact with social workers as a result of losses, deficits or radical changes in their circumstances. These may be accumulated gradually or may occur suddenly; and they may develop individually or in combination – the 'cluster of circumstances' (Saul, 1974). Most older people cope with such changes without social-work involvement but for a minority help is required. The situations which involve social workers in dealing with risks in the lives of older people will be considered in three broad contexts: situations needing urgent action, those involving personal help with feelings, attitudes and emotions, and those requiring the acquisition and provision of support in the community. These are not, of course, mutually exclusive.

IMMINENT AND SERIOUS DANGER: SITUATIONS WHERE URGENT ACTION IS NEEDED OR REQUESTED

An emergency may involve either the need for immediate action to avoid imminent danger or the need for an urgent response to deal with the effects of serious loss or damage after it has occurred. It should be recognized that a number of pressures may come to bear on the social worker to influence him to take action to ensure the safety of the older person. These pressures may sometimes be related as much or more to the anxieties of others as to the specific hazards to which the older person is exposed. Among the pressures may be the realistic fear of the consequences for the social worker if a disaster should occur when he could have taken preventive action. The exercise of professional judgment in an uncertain situation creates the possibility of guilt or blame, or the likelihood of censure by agency or colleagues, and even the possibility of formal inquiry or legal action. A further source of pressure derives from the generalized nature of much of the legislation relating to provision for older people. The lack of clearly established decision rules and guides increases the vulnerability felt by workers in resisting demands which they feel are inappropriate. A social worker will, for instance, find it difficult to resist the demand to provide residential accommodation if a hospital consultant suggests the older person does not require hospital treatment but is nevertheless unfit to be left in his own home. Further, the general lack of resources in the community can create pressure to admit frail, endangered older people to the assumed safety of residential or hospital care even though careful assessment may suggest the possibility of continuing care in the community.

Such pressure and, in particular, the anxieties and fears of
the carers or relatives at the time of decision making can lead
social workers into inappropriately hurried decision making.
Some of the issues involved in distinguishing the need for urgent
action from the pressure to take unnecessarily hurried action can
be illustrated.

Mr R (aged 75) was a widower living in a lodging house. The
social worker was asked to visit one evening by the proprietor
of the lodging house who requested the 'removal' or Mr R who
had kept the other residents up all the previous night by shouting and groaning and had appeared 'confused' all day. On visiting, the worker established that Mr R had no relatives living
near and was not registered with a GP. In the face of the proprietor's adamant insistence and in spite of Mr R's reluctance
the social worker arranged his immediate admission to a residential home.

After smashing up his room at the home and verbal aggression
to the staff, Mr R was admitted compulsorily to psychiatric hospital three days later. Following medical examination he was
found to be suffering from a severe respiratory infection and
to be undernourished. Following treatment for the infection and
good food and nursing care he was discharged to the same lodging house four weeks later. Arrangements were made for him to
attend a local day centre three times each week where he was
able to obtain regular meals.

In this situation the social worker, faced with strong pressure
to resolve a difficult situation, responded by removing Mr R to
alternative accommodation, although there were obvious indications of the need to seek medical advice. There was an undoubted
need to take urgent action but the hurried action taken was
clearly at variance with Mr R's needs and, as events eventually
showed, the action apparently aggravated the hazard and increased the risk to Mr R.

Urgent action, as a quick response to difficult situations, is
sometimes essential and is commonly dictated by the speed and
unexpectedness of the difficulty for the older person. The need
for urgent action in relation to an unanticipated emergency may
occur when there is a sudden loss of support for people living
alone who, without their usual supporters, are incapable of adequate self-care. Since the bulk of community care is provided
by people who have other commitments this is not uncommon. The
sudden incapacity of an older person who had previously been
able to function independently may also create imminent danger.
A slight stroke or fall may present acute difficulties, while not
necessitating hospital admission, and the older person's previous
ability to cope alone may mean there is no existing support network. Emergencies can also sometimes occur where any older
person is having difficulty with self-care but is not prepared to
accept the support that is available. Typical examples are the
locking out of home helps or neighbours, or the refusal to allow

them to make fires, cook food, etc. In the circumstances described here urgent need arises from the rapid deterioration or
sudden change of the older person, from the sudden loss of support, or from the sudden breakdown of the relationship between
the older person and his supporters.

The need for urgent action may also arise from the discovery
of an older person living in difficult and hazardous circum--
stances as the result of long-standing and progressive deterioration. An extreme, though not untypical example, will illustrate
this:

> Miss W, aged 83, lived alone in the middle of a housing estate
> in a densely populated urban area. She was referred to the
> Social Services' department as a result of frequent abortive
> visits by the Gas Board to obtain payment of an outstanding
> account. She had been seen moving about in the house which
> appeared dirty and neglected. When the social worker visited
> he was initially refused admission by Miss W and only on the
> fourth visit, with the help of a neighbour, was he able to gain
> admission. The house was found to be in an appalling condition,
> with food and rubbish everywhere and a number of dead cats
> in evidence. Urgent action was taken because of the risk to
> the health of Miss W and her neighbours.

This situation had developed over a considerable period and it
is, again, not uncommon to encounter older people who have been
determined to remain independent of others but who have therefore had no one to give support especially when their deteriorating circumstances reach extreme levels.

Perhaps one of the most difficult situations in which social
workers become involved in taking urgent action is when older
people are found wandering, often at night-time, and who are
unaware of the reality of their surroundings or of what is hap-
pening to them. Such situations are particularly difficult for the
social worker because of the pressure that is felt or is placed on
him to 'make safe' the older person - particularly if there are no
obvious carers or supporters available.

Urgent action is obviously not only indicated when older people
are living on their own. There is no doubt that some families
caring for older relatives do tolerate situations of considerable
difficulty and stress because of their acceptance of their responsibility to provide care (Harbert, 1978). Such families often do
not ask for help until they have reached or gone beyond the
point of breakdown. Often this is manifest in a refusal by the
family to carry on looking after the older person or occasionally
when difficulties are reported by others outside the family because of neglect or ill-treatment of the older person. It should
not be assumed that families refusing to provide for their older
relatives are uncaring: most frequently it is precisely their determination to continue looking after their relatives for as long
as possible which leads to the extreme strain and demand for
urgent help.

Some emergencies are completely unpredictable – fire, flood, gas explosions, etc. – and whether or not urgent action is needed will depend on a complex of factors. Other urgent needs can be anticipated and action taken to prevent, reduce or otherwise prepare for the consequences: the death of a spouse after a long illness, or eviction following a protracted legal process, or discharge from hospital, etc. The stress of the event may be considerable, even with forewarning and, even though preparations are made, some immediate action must often be taken to provide support, alternative resources, etc. Hazards may still exist in consequence of difficulties in obtaining resources, or in getting the consent of the older person or his family to action, or in decision making, etc.

Of crucial importance in considering ways in which social workers can approach these kinds of situations is the initial assessment. Often problems which are presented as crises are made up not of the perceptions of the older client but of those of neighbours, relations and friends. The so-called crisis gathers momentum as the daughter talks to neighbours, who talk to the doctor, etc. The final problem definition may bear little relation to the reality of the situation (Brearley, 1978). Although the desirability of careful and detailed risk analysis is clear, there seems to be some reason to doubt whether this actually occurs. One survey of emergency admissions to residential care found that

the haste with which such admissions have to be made more often than not sets them apart from the planned procedures which should characterize the admission process. This, in turn, frequently leads to inadequate evaluations of the alternative caring strategies. As a result many men and women who might properly have remained in the community, if not in their own homes, are summarily and unnecessarily placed in homes for the elderly (Pope, 1980, p. 18).

Although assessments may have to be made quickly, they should nevertheless be as full and careful as possible. Together with the older person and other people involved the social worker should compare the risks in the status quo with the risks of alternative courses of action. It is particularly important to guard against the hazard of incomplete information – well illustrated earlier in the case of Mr R.

Detailed risk analysis, then, is crucial and should be carried out with a high level of sensitivity and skill and an awareness of the pressures and pitfalls which may hinder proper assessment. The main elements of appropriate assessment have been outlined in Chapter 3: identifying current problems and hazards; measuring current strengths, including functional abilities, existing social supports and adaptive capabilities; assessing the environment and potential strengths and resources; and balancing likelihood against the value of consequences. Even in emergency the importance of involving the experience and knowledge of different professional groups should not be neglected. It may sometimes, for instance, be more appropriate to seek assessment in a hospital setting before admission to residential care is considered (see, for example, Brocklehurst et al., 1978).

Once an initial assessment has been made a range of possibilities is available to the social worker but the chosen response will, of course, vary with each situation and it is not possible to prescribe ideal solutions. However, in most situations of unexpected or sudden danger it may often be possible to offset immediate hazards, at least in the short term, either by providing adequate domiciliary support using statutory or formal volunteer organizations or by mobilizing help from friends, family and neighbours. The preferable goal of urgent action will be to achieve an acceptable level of safety in the community: at least to buy time, providing not only safety but a feeling of security for the older person and creating space for the social worker to complete an over-all evaluation. This will not always be possible and it will sometimes be necessary to arrange alternative accommodation in residential care or in hospital, via a doctor. Occasionally, action may be taken using compulsory powers under the 1959 Mental Health Act, or action may be initiated through the Community Physician under section 47 of the 1948 National Assistance Act (see Norman, 1979, for a detailed criticism of the use of compulsory powers).

Sometimes, of course, it will not be necessary to take any immediate action and it seems important to stress that any urgent action that is taken should not inhibit or preclude further intervention. It may be possible, even in situations of imminent family breakdown, for the social worker not only to contain the immediate distress but also to show the potential for future help – although people may often not be able to accept such possibilities. Often a social worker's visit can be sufficient to prevent immediate breakdown if families are sensitively given the opportunity to talk about their situation, to express their feelings, and to discuss the options that are realistically available to them. It will be appropriate to consider the possibilities of practical help and relief – day care to provide tangible relief, for example, may offer sufficient support to enable carers to take time to review alternative ways of coping and prevent precipitate admission to residential care.

Sometimes removal from the hazardous situations will be unavoidable but urgent action means neither that the general guiding principles for practice outlined earlier should be neglected, nor that the quality of social work involvement is diluted for reasons of haste. Rather it calls for a heightened and sharpened approach, demanding a view of the future needs of the older person as well as the short-term problems. The provision of immediate domiciliary support and efficient, practical support systems is essential but represents only a part of the need. At a time when reaction to loss may be acute and feelings of distress and

disorientation are common older people are particularly in need
of concerned and sensitive counselling help. It should also be
remembered that urgent situations are not necessarily entirely
negative. It has long been recognized that at times of stress and
crisis there is potential for positive adaptation. The actions
taken by the social worker can have a very significant effect
both in offsetting hazards but also in laying the foundations for
growth and helpful change.

RESPONDING TO LOSS: PERSONAL HELP WITH FEELINGS,
ATTITUDES AND EMOTIONS

The main focus here is on situations where the nature of social-
work involvement is governed by the need to provide help principally for the older person himself with emotional difficulties or
dangers occurring as a result of loss, or in association with
decision making in situations which could result in loss. Two
areas will be highlighted by way of example: help with dying and
bereavement and admissions to residential care, where the help
given is primarily geared towards personal problem solving in
relation to feelings, attitudes and emotions, as well as practical
services.
   Many people who are dying appreciate the opportunity to discuss their feelings with a sympathetic listener (Hinton, 1967)
and many writers have stressed the importance of creating a cli-
mate in which the individual feels free to discuss his feelings
about his pending death (see, for example, Kubler-Ross 1973).
Social-work literature has indicated many ways in which social
workers might help the dying (see, for example Holden, 1979).
Much of this help will be of a counselling nature, in which the
social worker, like doctors and nurses caring for the terminally
ill, takes part in 'a process of psychological transition which,
like grief, requires time, empathy and trust' (Parkes, 1972,
p. 179). The social worker can help both the dying person and
his relatives reach a stage where they can acknowledge reality
and make sensible plans for the survivor. There is evidence to
suggest that this can bring relief to the dying and relatives alike
(Parkes, 1972). The kind of situation which is most likely to be
brought to the social worker's attention, in relation to death and
dying, is that of an older person attempting to care for a dying
spouse or relative in circumstances where there is physical as
well as emotional stress present. As many older people choose to
die in their own homes rather than in hospital, and their relatives often wish to care for them in this setting (or have no
choice but to do so), this can frequently involve a great deal of
hard work and consequent emotional stress for the carer. In
these circumstances the social worker can, as well as offering
emotional support, ease the physical burden of the carer with
the provision of a range of domiciliary services, such as domestic
laundry services, night sitters, and home helps, which may, by

relieving tiredness and demonstrating tangible evidence of concern, give the carer strength to cope with the impending loss
and its aftermath.

The effects of bereavement can also bring older people into
contact with social workers. Before discussing the ways in which
social workers can help the bereaved, some of the things we
understand about grief can be outlined. The normal psychological reaction to loss of any important aspect of life is grief and
there is a general consensus that there is a normal process of
grieving; that is, that grief follows a predictable course (see,
for example, Parkes, 1972). Most authors would agree that normal grief is composed of different stages, and although precise
categorizations of these stages differ, most also agree that typical grief reactions produce a cluster of symptoms by which we
can identify a 'general syndrome of grief'. In the usual course
of events the bereaved person will pass through these stages as
he (or, more frequently, she) continues to do the work of mourning and to cope with the many memories associated with the dead
person. This process will slowly subside over weeks and months
until he is able to begin investing energy and interest in other
people to replace the lost one. As Parkes says 'Grief is a process of realisation and "making real" the fact of loss' (1972,
p. 183). The assumption is that those who are able to move
through the various stages of grief will then be freed to get on
with 'normal' life.

There is some evidence to suggest, however, that grief may
take an 'atypical' form which will occur when there is a disruption or a distortion of this process (Gramlich, 1973). Two
categorizations of atypical grief seem particularly relevant to
older people: inhibited and chronic grief. Inhibited grief occurs
in individuals in whom mourning seems to be subdued but in
whom it is long lasting and associated with disturbed behaviour
or physical symptoms. Chronic grief is a prolongation and inten-
sification of the normal grief process and may be associated with
overt somatic pain and distress. If an older person is suffering
from a grief reaction, he is less likely to show overt signs of
emotional distress, but his grief may be characterized by physical complaints and may well adopt a devious pattern (Parkes,
1972).

It is common for the immediate carers and family of the bereaved, as well as the older person himself, to need information
which will enable them to recognize the normality of some of the
symptoms displayed. The social worker can also help the older
person, and help the carers to assist him by accepting and encouraging them to accept feelings of hostility and anger, by
encouraging weeping in the initial stages, by refusing to probe
the older person's feelings and not attempting to jolly him out of
his misery, by helping him to arrange things in whatever way is
necessary to set him free for the task of grieving, and by providing reassurances that some of the alarming concomitants of
grief, sometimes even hallucinations, are not evidence that he is

losing his reason (Parkes, 1972). The social worker, in doing this, will be creating the conditions which will allow grief to progress and not to be disrupted or distorted. An example of an older person who was helped in this way can be given:

Mr M, aged 67, was bereaved after 45 years of marriage. Shortly after his wife's death, he moved temporarily into his daughter's household, 'to give him time to get over it'. The social worker was asked to visit by the daughter's general practitioner because she had visited him in some distress as her father was being verbally abusive. This occurred some weeks after Mrs M had died. The general practitioner identified Mr M's changed behaviour as a grief response, and felt that both Mr M and his daughter needed help in this situation. The social worker held five interviews with Mr M following a joint interview with Mr M, his daughter and son-in-law, and it emerged that the daughter in particular had been, albeit kindly, attempting to get Mr M to make decisions about his own home and various financial matters. She agreed to desist from this for the time being. This eased the stress in the situation, primarily because the daughter could now understand Mr M's aggression, and Mr M himself felt that he had benefited from the opportunity of expressing his feelings to the social worker.

The social worker helped the process along and the case does illustrate two important points. Important decisions should not be taken in the early stages of grief, for example, decisions about accommodation (British Association of Social Workers, 1977). Similarly, anything that forces the bereaved person to confront reality before he is ready can give rise to difficulties (Parkes, 1972).

It has been argued that grief can present atypically among older people and Parkes also stresses that helpers should pay particular attention to 'the absence of grief in situations where it would have been expected, episodes of panic, lasting physical symptoms, excessive guilt feelings, excessive anger, or the persistence of intense grief beyond the normally expected period' (p. 192). The social worker, in recognizing atypical reactions, should always consider whether there is a need for specialist psychiatric help and be aware of some of the 'risks' involved for the bereaved older person. It is important to anticipate the chance of the older person becoming depressed and possibly suicidal. Research has shown that a high proportion of older people who complete suicide suffer from a definite psychiatric illness, usually depression (Harbridge, 1980b), and the possibility of both bereavement and depression as indicators of suicidal potential has been noted (Resnik and Cantor, 1973).

It seems important, when counselling the bereaved and the depressed older person, to note the value of what has been called Life Review therapy. This has developed from the assertion

that reminiscence in older people is not psychologically dysfunc-
tional or a symptom of waning mental faculties, but a progressive
return to consciousness of past experiences in which the resur-
gence of unresolved conflicts can be surveyed and reintegrated.
McMahon and Rhudick have stressed that reminiscing should be
encouraged as 'it is positively related to freedom from depression
and personal survival' (1967, p. 78). Butler has endorsed this
view and has shown how the tendency and ability to reminisce
can be consciously harnessed. He argues that many older people
can be helped to conduct their own life review and that this can
be effectively used to help them come to terms with present difficulties (1963, 1975).

Whatever counselling techniques or methods are used in dealing
with the bereaved older person, it seems clear that the approach
should not be a completely narcissistic exercise for the older person. It has been suggested that the goal of casework with the
grieving older person is to 'reinforce and strengthen his capacity
to cope with his environment and to regain his sense of control
and mastery' (Wasser, 1966, p. 81). It is also important to emphasize the need for the bereaved to develop new relationships
to replace lost ones (Parkes, 1972). The social worker, then,
should focus attention not only on feelings about loss, but also
on relationships and interactions within the community.

Finally, helping an older person to come to terms with his bereavement involves the social worker sharing the pain and, to be
able to do this, the social worker's own capacity to cope with his
own losses and his reactions to death, dying and grieving are
crucial. Wasser has pointed out that unless the social worker has
come to terms with these areas in his own life 'exposure to the
pain of a grieving client can cause unconscious negative reactions
in a worker, which may lead him to avoid or withdraw from the
sensitive area' (p. 83). Leared, more positively, sees the social
worker's own feelings as a tool in the helping process: 'knowing
about our own fears of loss gives us strength to contain other
people's fears and pain' (1978).

Grief is commonly associated with the loss of a person, but it
should be noted that grief has been recognized as a reaction to
many other forms of loss (Parkes, 1972; Marris, 1974). Loss of
environment can be as critical for an older person as the loss of
a close relative or partner might be for another. The decision
about whether to apply for or accept residential care is one which
warrants close attention and is an area where the social worker
is involved in dealing with the anxieties and worries of older
people and, in some cases, of their families or carers.

Research has suggested that in addition to the general risks to
older people which may occur following admission to residential
care, such as an increased risk of infection, there are specific
indications of vulnerable groups in this context. Older people
with an habitually passive approach to life are more vulnerable
to a negative outcome following admission (Yawney and Slover,
1973), as are those with a marked degree of brain failure, illness

or physical decline. The degree of choice older people have about accepting residential care is important to successful outcome (Noelker and Harel, 1978), as is also the degree of change in environment: the more moderate the change, the less marked the effect may be (Gutman and Herbert, 1976).

Moreover, there is evidence to suggest that moving from one environment to another is in itself stressful and predictive of physical deterioration. In one American study it was shown that those who stay transitionally in nursing homes before final admission are particularly vulnerable to negative outcomes (Tobin and Lieberman, 1976).

Hence, it is reasonable to argue that admission to residential care can sometimes create more problems for the older person than it solves. Admission to care should therefore be the subject of careful and well-informed decision making. There is a clear responsibility on social workers dealing with requests for residential accommodation to ensure that the possible negative consequences of admission are presented as well as the positive reasons for admission. The social worker has a crucially important role in helping older people reach the stage where they can make an informed decision about residential care. This can be done in a number of ways. In addition to supplying verbal information, the social worker can use the residential resource imaginatively to help in the decision making process, by enabling the older person to visit the home, or by providing day care for a limited period at the home, so that he can obtain a clearer idea of what life in that establishment means. If this is impractical or undesirable for any reason, it should be possible to arrange for one of the care staff to visit him in his own home to establish contact and to give the necessary detailed information to the older person. The older person will, of course, be interested in practical issues as well as philosophies of residential care: how much he will have to pay, how finances are administered, whether he will retain his pension book, what will happen to his personal possessions, whether he will have a room to himself, etc. Information of this detailed nature is essential if the decision is to be a meaningful one.

Not only is it important for the social worker to inform the client of alternatives to residential care and to provide them where requested, but he must also attempt to ensure that the older person makes the decision unencumbered by pressure, either from himself or others involved, although it may be the social worker's task in certain situations to ensure that the older person realistically appreciates the views and attitudes of people who are also involved in the situation.

Not only can the social worker help in the actual decision-making process, but he can also help the older person prepare for admission once the decision to enter care has been reached. There is some evidence to suggest that careful preparation and planning for the move may minimize many of the harmful effects of admission (Pablo, 1977). Again, full and detailed information about objectives and expectations will reduce stress on admission (Spasoff et al., 1978). Particularly important is the relationship between the older person feeling abandoned and separated and a negative outcome to admission (Tobin and Lieberman, 1976). Counselling of the older person and his family, to help them discuss and face the nature and inevitability of changes, may reduce the possibility of a negative reaction to admission, and any feelings of guilt or neglect which close relatives may feel as a result of their inability to support an older person at home.

It is important for the social worker to recognize that despite the older person seeming to make the decision to enter residential care rationally and with an acceptance that it is the only sensible course of action to take, he may still have many doubts, fears, and negative expectations about residential care. These must be recognized and dealt with (Noelker and Harel, 1978). The worker should also be aware that the decision to enter care is in itself an important trigger to behavioural change. Withdrawn and self-centred behaviour are features of the waiting period for admission, as much as of living in residential care (Tobin and Lieberman, 1976). Part of the preparation must also focus on preparing the residential establishment to receive the older person and, above all, it is particularly important that support is provided at the time of admission (Brearley et al., 1980).

This brief review of two aspects of counselling with older people, in the context of bereavement, decision making and admission to care, is intended to be illustrative of some of the ways in which social workers can offer help to older people and their families. There are many other situations in which similar help is appropriate and it seems essential that people who are exposed to a variety of hazards should have access to social-work help. Such help will be needed with both practical needs and the emotional response to those needs and there is ample evidence that counselling help can be effective when carefully and purposefully given in selected situations. There are, of course, a range of possible approaches to helping in social work and it seems as appropriate to consider these in relation to older people as any other group. Mention is made elsewhere in this book of the application of behavioural principles in the reality-orientation approach, for example; similarly, the relevance of task-centred and goal-orientated approaches has been noted and approaches to family therapy and family casework are likely to be important in the total repertoire of resources. It is, in other words, necessary to take a broad and creative view of potential counselling approaches.

So far we have considered two kinds of risk situations: those in which danger is imminent and grave and urgent action is necessary, and those in which the older person is exposed to emotional risks. A further set of situations are those in which risks are of a chronic, or longer term nature. Some people continue to live in the community only because of the support and help given by others, and without which they would be in considerable danger. The primary issues for these older people centre on the effective provision of what is generally called community care to offset hazards.

MAINTENANCE AND PROTECTION: ACQUIRING AND PROVIDING COMMUNITY SUPPORT

It was shown in Chapter 3 that there is potentially a range of informal support available to older people in addition to the help which can be given by professional agencies. The flexible and innovative use of statutory resources in combination with the informal community resources of family, friends and volunteers provides the basis for care and support. Obviously the degree of help required and the range of support given will vary according to a number of factors, including the physical and mental condition of the older person, his social and domestic situation and his subjective appreciation of this, and the extent and reliability of existing support. The help given can range from the provision of domiciliary services to older people who still retain skills, despite deficiencies in some areas of functioning, such as cooking and shopping, to a carefully thought out and implemented package of services to meet a multiplicity of needs. It should, of course, be remembered that the use of services to maintain and protect older people can actually have the effect of increasing dependency and therefore undermining the basic objective of increasing competence and the fit between need and environment (see, for example, Blenkner, 1966; Blenkner et al., 1971). Some central issues can be illustrated:

> Miss J, aged 72, lived alone in a small cottage in a village. Her only living relative was her 70-year-old brother, who lived with his sick wife, in the next village, four miles away. Miss J has been diagnosed by a psychiatrist on a domiciliary visit as suffering from senile dementia and had, for some time, become progressively less able to wash and dress herself properly, make and light the coal fire in her cottage, attend to her shopping and eating needs and manage her finances. She had begun to take to her bed for part of the day, and occasionally to wander around the house at night, and on one occasion, was returned home by a neighbour after wandering out into the lanes around her cottage in the early hours of the morning. The psychiatrist did not feel that admission to hospital was appropriate, but was concerned about the level of care Miss J was receiving and about the stresses placed upon her brother who was visiting her for increasingly lengthy periods each day. Miss J was being cared for by a combination of home help and meals on wheels on three days a week each, plus the support given by her brother.

The social worker who visited Miss J felt that the existing level of support was inadequate to meet her needs and consequently the home help's hours were increased and varied so that she visited for one hour at lunch-time each day to cook a meal for Miss J, and as a secondary task to keep the cottage tidy. She also prepared sandwiches for her to eat at tea-time. Meals on wheels were discontinued as Miss J rarely ate them anyway. A district nurse was contacted, via the general practitioner, to help get Miss J up in the mornings and dressed, and to give her a regular bath. The neighbour was approached and agreed to call in to see Miss J for an hour each evening, to help her get organised for bed and to ensure that she was in bed safely before leaving. For this she was paid under a good neighbour scheme. Miss J's brother, released from many of the basic caring tasks he had previously undertaken and the problems of thrice daily journeys between his own home and Miss J's, began to visit just once a day, usually at a time when no one else was present, which he spent talking to her and occasionally taking her out for short walks.

It is possible to use this example to illustrate some of the functions of the social worker in this kind of situation. The social worker assessed the hazards and dangers to Miss J and the other individual mainly affected - her brother - and concluded that she needed additional care to ensure her safety, and physical well-being in the community. Both he and Miss J felt that she should remain in her own home, and that she could be maintained with a package of services, which would at the same time relieve some of the stress on her brother. In this case, the hazards which needed attention were reasonably clear, but assessing and providing community care will not always be so straightforward. A useful concept to consider in this context is that of social network analysis which emphasizes the value of social support to the functioning and adaptation of the individual, especially in times of crisis when supportive relationships can lessen the effects of stress (Boswell, 1969). Network therapy has been used effectively to bring into the information gathering and decision-making processes anyone in the community who has some knowledge of an individual, as a basis for gathering information and motivating support within the community (Cresswell, 1977). It can therefore provide a framework for a comprehensive assessment of an older person's needs, in terms of the need for a 'minimum sufficient network' for basic social survival and satisfaction.

In Miss J's case the social worker provided domiciliary support in the form of increasing the home help, and acquired the services of the good neighbour; this gives an example of the way in which support from the formal sector can be combined with help from the informal sector. The distinction made between help provided and help acquired in this way is an important one. The acquisition of help from the community is a complex matter and

the relationship between the formal and informal caring sectors
is often difficult. This may be because the motivation for helping
is essentially different. The basis for most informal care is re-
ciprocity: 'help and care are so often given neither for material
reward nor philanthropic motive, but because there is an existing relationship within which exchanges of care and support
have already taken place through natural social procession'
(Parker, 1978).

The attempt to utilize natural helpers can flounder because
the helpers are not willing to conform to, or are anxious about,
the local authority's expectations of them and their role and perhaps feel that a change in their relationship to the older person
or their presence as agents of the local authority in the older
person's home would be detrimental to their relationship. It is
likely that to utilize neighbourhood help effectively the social
worker may have to fit in with the priorities and conventions of
the community rather than merely those of his agency. The more
effective approach may well be to accept what the informal helper
is prepared to offer the older person on his or her own terms,
and, if necessary, to supplement this help with the provision of
formal resources, thereby opting for co-existence rather than
attempting to control the informal help.

In the case of Miss J the social worker also co-ordinated the
various supporters and functioned as an information receiver and
disseminator between them. The importance of one person accepting the responsibility for co-ordinating activity and ensuring
that relevant information is disseminated to other people concerned is well documented in the child-care field and is equally
important for dealings with older people. In the case of Miss J
the social worker co-ordinated services to ensure that they were
not duplicated, at particular points in time, and especially to ensure that there were no critical gaps in service delivery.

In many situations it is necessary for the social worker to provide support for the carers of old people. There is ample evidence
that caring for older people can have harmful effects on the
carers themselves and on their own families, manifested by, for
example, marital strife and breakdown, chronic misery and even
loss of income (Hawks, 1975). This is perhaps particularly relevant where older people are living with their families, creating
situations where action is needed to relieve the stress:

> Mrs D, aged 69, was widowed and lived with her son-in-law
> and daughter and their two teenage children in their small
> semi-detached house. A great deal of friction was caused by
> Mrs D's objection to the children playing 'pop records' and
> being generally noisy, and the children's embarrassment, and
> subsequent refusal to invite their friends to their home, be-
> cause of their grandmother's unpleasant dribbling and eating
> habits caused by a slight stroke. Mrs D's daughter, torn be-
> tween her loyalty to her mother and to her own family, became
> increasingly unable to tolerate the many disagreements which

were developing between herself and her husband about the difficulties. This situation was ameliorated by providing day care at a centre for Mrs D at week-ends, when the children most wanted to relax and to bring their friends into the home (a solution which also pleased Mrs D) and the provision of two weeks' short-term care in a residential home, which enabled the rest of the family to take a holiday together.

Sometimes in such situations there is a danger that the older person may be scapegoated and become the focal point of all the family's difficulties or, alternatively, may involve the family in many of his own personal difficulties. In such cases more sophisticated counselling-based responses may be required. However, it is more common for social workers to become involved in situations where the hazards are primarily practical with associated emotional stresses, and in situations where caring for an older person raises a number of emotional and perhaps moral issues for adult children. In this context it is worth noting the value of short-term counselling groups for children coping with elderly parents, and there is some evidence to suggest that an informal supportive approach of this nature is effective in helping adult children make decisions and act on them (Hausman, 1979).

One other role commonly adopted by social workers is in relation to the monitoring and surveillance of those older people in the community who are likely to deteriorate or come to harm unless someone keeps an eye on them. What evidence there is suggests that social workers, if only because of the constraints of time, are unable to fulfil this function adequately: 'it became obvious that the occasional social work visit was not the most appropriate means of providing support or of anticipating approaching crises' (Goldberg and Warburton, 1979, p. 284). Only frequent and consistent contact with an older person can provide surveillance in any meaningful way; home helps, workers in sheltered accommodation, district nurses and local network groups are more consistent and frequent visitors to the homes of the older population than are social workers. It would therefore seem more appropriate for the social worker, when he has reason to suspect possible deterioration in the circumstances of older people, to link into and establish clear channels of communication with existing contacts in order to give him adequate information and warning of impending difficulties for the older person. The establishment and clarification of clear referral routes can provide a more comprehensive monitoring system than social workers alone can hope to provide.

Despite the emphasis that has been given to support that can be made available to older people within the community, and the needs of those providing this support, it is obviously extremely important, as we highlighted at the beginning of this chapter, not to forget the rights and needs of the older person in this situation. Community care will break down unless the older person himself sees his helpers in a positive light, and his rights to choose how he wishes to live must be respected and balanced against the need to protect and support. The dangers to the rights of older people are considerable and the reader is recommended to consider the issues raised by Norman (1979) in her discussion document on rights, risk and older people.

GROUPS AND OLDER PEOPLE

Before concluding this chapter some references must also be made to the use of groups in social work with older people. Comparatively little has been written about social work with older people in groups, although this situation is slowly beginning to change as more emphasis is put on the use of group-care facilities, other than in institutions. One element of the relative lack of interest in group-work approaches to older people is the generally negative and oversimplified assumptions made about work with this group. A more practical and realistic reason is the difficulty of getting older people together, since those with whom social workers are likely to be involved are also those who are most likely to be isolated by mobility difficulties. Not only is it difficult and expensive to bring such older people together, but also problems of communication arise because of the higher probability of sensory loss. In spite of these apparent difficulties older people do come together for many different reasons - leisure, education, decision making, political action, companionship, treatment, care, etc. Social workers become involved in such groups in many settings but for the purposes of this brief review some of the objectives of groups for older people will be discussed and related particularly to day care and residential settings, and to the recent growth in community self-help groups.

Leisure and activity groups
The great majority of older people are not involved in formal groups. A national survey found that almost 64 per cent of people over the age of 65 are not members of any voluntary organization, including active church membership (Hunt, 1978). Clubs especially for older people are also only of significance to a small proportion (12.8 per cent of the over 75s and 8.6 per cent of those 65 to 74 years (Abrams, 1978). However, such clubs do become of increasing importance with age and are particularly significant for those people who are living alone. Most groups of older people are run by retired people and offer a wide range of different leisure activities. Generally they do not involve social-work activity, unless specific community-work objectives are identified: we will return to this a little later.

The increase in the amount of leisure-time available in retirement has made it possible for more people to become involved in education and the encouragement of older people to become involved in educational provision is very important to continued satisfaction. Jones (1976) has argued that learning activity is therapeutic because it helps to build a sense of progress and mastery through seeing the results of one's own effort and because 'progressive experience of the results of one's own efforts innoculates a person against the helplessness which can lead to depression' (p. 48).

This view can be linked with those approaches which stress the importance of physical activity to continuing health and well-being. It has been widely argued that there is a connection between 'meaningful leisure' which helps to keep the mind active and physical activity which helps to maintain active and positive health (Mack, 1980). This again may range from craftwork in day centres, to exercises in groups (Davies, 1975) and to dancing and other physical activities. It has been reported that Age Concern, Newcastle, hold regular disco-dancing sessions in their premises with great success (Mack, 1980).

Self-help groups
The importance to social work of the group activities so far described may be indirect but the imaginative use of leisure and the maintenance of activity both for the mind and body are fundamental aspects of using groups for older people. These aspects form one element in the growth of self-help among older people in recent years. A number of other threads or strands also contribute to the self-help approach: the importance of sharing of skills and resources, the extension of opportunities, and above all the need for older people to play a part in decision making processes that affect their lives. Self-help is a term that has had growing usage in many aspects of social work but it was only in the early 1970s that it began to be developed in relation to older people. At that time developments were tentative and based on two general assumptions. First, that in institutional settings and other groups older people could be involved and therefore gain some control over decision making and relearn and develop skills and, second, that in the community they could also begin to meet some of the needs which were not being met by existing services (Brearley (ed.), 1975b). Since then approaches to self-help have become more developed, particularly in relation to health-care groups (Katz and Bender, 1976; Robinson and Henry, 1977). Self-help groups among older people have been divided into those started spontaneously by older people themselves, such as the National Federation of Old Age Pensioners' Associations (begun in 1938) and the British Pensioners Trade Unions' Action Committee and most social clubs for the retired, and those which are initiated by an 'outside' worker (Blaire, 1978).

Some groups have been concerned mainly with providing fresh role opportunities for older people, ranging from leadership and political activist roles to support and companionship roles. There are a number of reports of group developments in institutional settings which fall into this category. A report of a programme in a small long-stay geriatric hospital, for example, identified the

primary needs of patients to feel a part of what was done to and
for them and also to have a degree of choice. The way of meeting
these objectives was to experiment with a range of alternative
role experiences made available to patients. Discussion groups,
activity groups and opportunities to participate in staff discussion groups were made available to extend the social opportunities and involvement of patients. The project particularly noted
that, in a situation where it has been generally accepted that
older patients will function at a very inactive level, it is important to provide an initial stimulus, and the project experience
suggests that this will generate some initial hostility and confusion for patients and staff (Brearley and Richardson, 1975).
Although some have argued that self-help activity is usually
brought about by a common problem or crisis, there is often a
need for a social worker to act as a catalyst or enabler to stimulate group activity. There is a precarious borderline between
stimulating or enabling, and being directive: the difference between helping people to help themselves and doing things for
them.

Other self-help groups have developed primarily to enable
older people to share their existing skills and resources with
each other. Reference was made earlier to the growth of small
group living schemes in residential care which provide one example of this approach. The concept is equally relevant in the
community setting. The Link Opportunity scheme was originally
seen as a job-swapping scheme for retired people (Brearley,
1978). The scheme has been developed in a number of ways and
some approaches have emphasized the volunteer input rather
than the self-help aspect: this is partly because of the potential
imbalance of skills and services. Many older people need help
with gardening, decorating, etc., but relatively few are able to
offer these services and it is necessary to seek involvement of
younger people to meet this demand.

A further element of the self-help approach stresses the importance of older people playing a part in decision making. Once
again this can be demonstrated in many settings, ranging from
the development of residents' committees in residential settings
to such organizations as the Tooting Action for Pensioners Group.
The latter organization began in 1972 and is now self-sufficient:
it has no committee but everyone is reported to participate
actively. One of its most successful campaigns involved the production of a dossier on the state of paving-stones in the local
borough which led to the immediate repair of the pavements
(Blaire, 1978). Throughout the 1970s self-help grew from a concept to an active social movement in the United Kingdom, although
primarily in the London area. This seems to have very important
implications for social-work approaches. Task Force, a voluntary
group working mainly in London, has played a particularly important part in developing community groups. A review of some
of the projects in which it has been involved (Buckingham et al.,
1979) outlines some of the aims of community work with pensioners,
who would have:

1 greater control
    (a) over the groups or clubs to which they belong;
    (b) over areas outside their groups which affect them
        e.g. access to local resources, such as social services,
        welfare benefits;
    (c) over decisions which affect their lives ...
2 greater opportunity to develop their own creativity;
3 greater opportunity to be and feel useful;
4 greater opportunity to get to know other people;
5 greater opportunity to combat ageism (p. 18)

There is no apparent reason to believe that these aims are not equally appropriate in forms of total care - hospitals and residential homes. Older people, wherever they are, have a right to be involved and a need to remain active, and social workers have a role to play in ensuring that they get, or make for themselves, the necessary opportunities.

Individual change and growth and the group process
Two general approaches to groups of older people have been discussed so far: those concerned with leisure, education and activity, and those concerned with promoting self-help in its broadest sense. A third approach concentrates on individual growth, change, or treatment in the group.

Some reference has already been made to Reality Orientation as a way of helping older people to recover skills and to keep in touch with the world by reducing confused behaviour. This may also be seen in the context of what has been called milieu-therapy, involving a total approach to improving the environment. A description of a residential home in Leicestershire, for instance, stresses the importance of 'natural living' in improving the quality of life for residents. This includes giving a continuity of life-style for people entering the home, sharing and taking responsibility, establishing a residents' committee, tailoring meal times, bed times, etc. to individual life-styles, providing work and educational opportunities and emphasizing orientation and resident participation in decision making (Dunphy and Lodge, 1979). One way of perceiving group living, then, is to stress the quality of the over-all environment in providing for individual continuity and growth.

Other approaches have been concerned with personal counselling through the group process (see, for example, Heymann, 1974) and others have developed a variety of therapeutic approaches (see, for example, Butler, 1960; Finkel and Fillmore, 1971; Lazarus, 1976). The objectives of these groups vary but have been concerned with such things as resocialization, increasing social contact among patients, increasing verbalization of feelings, and improving diagnostic evaluations and active treatment. Most reports note improvement in some of these aspects but the variables involved are very diverse and, as with Reality Orientation, it is difficult to relate change to specific

group activity. One general issue noted in several studies is
the importance of involving all staff in group-work planning in
institutions because of the possibility of conflict and confusion.
It may be that change following the introduction of group-work
into such situations is less the result of group activities than
the over-all impact on staff attitudes and behaviour towards
groups which develops in association with the incorporation of
group-work.

There are, of course, many different approaches to group-
work and these cannot be explored here, particularly as there is
relatively little evidence, either based on research or experience
with older people. One useful small-scale study attempted to distinguish two main themes or models of group-work with older
people. The first was described as the 'Here and Now' model
based on the philosophy of learning theorists which suggests
that a focus on either the past or the future encourages the
avoidance of dealing adaptively with problems in the present.
The second, the 'There and Then' model, propounded particularly
by Butler (1963, 1975) and by Lewis and Butler (1974), emphasizes the importance of the past and of using a life-review orientation. Comparing two groups, each using one of these two
models, the authors of the study found some progress was made
in each group but suggest that each approach is useful for some
people but not for others. The study is most useful for its clarification of these two approaches, although it does demonstrate
that group therapy can be an effective approach with older
people (Ingersoll and Silverman, 1978). Similarly, Cooper's sensitive report of group-work in a hospital setting gives vivid
confirmation of the value of group discussions to older people
(Cooper, 1980).

From this brief review it should be clear that groups can and
should be an important part of the lives of many older people
and that there is a role for social workers in three broad areas:

1 Ensuring that all older people have access to a range of
  leisure, education and activity groups.
2 Stimulating and supporting self-help activities through
  group involvement in the community and in institutional and
  day-care settings.
3 Providing group-counselling opportunities.

In these terms group-work can contribute to broadening opportunity, ability and resilience and therefore to reducing over-all
risk while at the same time it has a part to play in meeting needs
and managing individual risk. Once again, effective group-work
involves a recognition of the importance of risk taking to a quality of life. As the Personal Social Services Council have commented, 'acceptance of risk is fundamental to good residential
care, both for the resident and for the staff' (1977, para. 1.17).
The principle applies equally to all contexts of living.

CONCLUDING

There is no apparent reason to believe that the demands made
by work with older clients are substantially less than those of
work with other groups. Such work is no easier and no less
stressful and indeed, since work with older people is likely to
involve life-and-death decisions, it can be more stressful for the
worker than many other situations. Social work with older people
should be concerned with offering individual solutions in a flexible way. Each person grows old in his own particular way and
although most people do not find old age a time of insurmountable problems a substantial minority do need help to overcome a
wide variety of hazards, deficiencies and accumulated losses.

In this chapter we have set out some basic principles and
issues for practice, and have explored some aspects of social-
work practice in relation to the need for urgent action, personal
counselling, longer term supportive needs and the use of groups
with older people. In concluding we would stress again the importance of detailed and careful assessment and risk analysis,
of constructing flexible packages of care to meet individual needs,
and of providing a balance between provision of practical services and the meeting of relationship needs. The hazards to
older people are both practical and emotional and although the
priority for most will be the meeting of material needs, the provision of a counselling service is as appropriate to the needs of
older people as it is to other groups.

Further, it must be recognized that effective help can sometimes only be given in the knowledge that it involves a degree
of risk. This is both in the sense that much action with older
people takes place in the context of uncertainty and also in the
sense that sometimes it is necessary to take a gamble – to put
something at stake in the hope of gaining a better quality of life.

5 RISK AND MENTAL DISORDER

Peter Jefferys and Rosemary Jennings

Mental disorder is common among older people, with at least one-fifth of the over 65s living in the community showing evidence of a serious mental disorder at any one time. The mentally ill older person is more likely to be receiving some form of personal social services than the mentally fit, and emergency or crisis presentation to social services or health service are frequent. Older people with mental illness exhibit high physical and social morbidity, and risk assessment and management will almost always include physical, behavioural or psychological and social components.

PROFESSIONAL CONTACTS

In the United Kingdom with its wide range of primary care services and agencies the problems of an older person with mental illness may initially be referred either to the health service or personal social services in a variety of ways. Referrals may be client or patient initiated, when, for example, a depressed woman believing she has bowel cancer seeks advice from her general practitioner. Or referrals may be made on behalf of the older person by a relative, neighbour or other carer, with relatives sometimes having needs and problems of their own, as with a husband confessing his fears of physically injuring his severely confused spouse and begging the duty social worker to intervene.

In practice, the general practitioner is the professional agency in the community most frequently consulted by older people and their families, with other primary carers such as the district nurse, health visitor, voluntary or church worker, police and social worker often drawing the doctors attention to behavioural change.

The general practitioner in his turn may seek specialist or secondary care assistance in his management of the mentally ill older person, with a referral to a consultant psychiatrist, or to a specialized local authority day-centre for the mentally ill or to social services with a request for residential care. Alternatively, or sometimes in addition, the general practitioner may involve other primary care workers such as district nurse, health visitor or a social worker requesting home help or meals on wheels or other social support.

On the other hand, the doctor may choose not to involve other professionals or to seek specialist help and will attempt to manage the mental problem himself or even try to ignore it and hope the problem will go away. The knowledge and understanding of mental illness by GPs is growing, but is still very patchy. Although they make more referrals to social services on behalf of older people than any other single agency, their knowledge and understanding of social-work practice is often sparse and the doctor's opinion about the social-work objective for an older client may differ radically from that of the social worker's. In addition, with many older mentally ill clients known to both the GP and social worker, neither professional involved may have a clear idea of what information needs communicating to the other or when or how. Unfortunately, sharing of essential social or clinical information about a mentally ill older person in the community between the GP and social worker rarely occurs as a matter of course. However, it would be uncommon for a social worker working with a mentally ill older client exposed to major dangers or hazards not to liaise with the GP, in contrast perhaps with more erratic communication in the opposite direction were referral initially to the doctor.

Social-work duty or in-take teams are less frequently the first professional contact for the older mentally ill, but social workers will often receive referrals when crises develop with an older person thought to be 'at risk', such referrals often being via other primary carers such as the GP, home help, volunteers or the police. In many urban areas hospital accident and emergency departments provide an out-of-hours service to which some older people in crisis are referred, bypassing the GP. The hospital emergency department may in its turn then refer the older person to emergency social-work services.

ASSESSMENT

An older person presenting with psychiatric symptoms to a social worker or GP requires assessment, which is a preliminary to the making of one or more clinical diagnoses coupled with the formulation of a social and dynamic picture and plans for subsequent management. Medical input is essential for new referrals, but all disciplines need to appreciate the over-all aims of assessment and the content and structure of the procedures used to achieve these aims.

Assessment structure
1 Clear history.
2 Physical examination.
3 Mental state examination.
4 Social/personal care/family support assessment.
5 Initial formulation or preliminary diagnosis.
6 Further investigation required.
7 Immediate/long-term management.

Assessment of the mentally ill older person is complex and challenging, with resemblances to a good 'who dunnit', requiring good detective work in following a range of clues and often requiring expert witnesses.

The history
A clear and ordered account must be obtained from interview with the older person of the current symptoms or problems, coupled with verification from other informants. Careful cross-questioning of the older person and informant will often be required to clarify the psychological, social or environmental variables linked with the development of their symptoms. The informant may include spouse, daughter or other relative, neighbour or church worker, district nurse, health visitor or GP, home help, meals on wheels driver or the police. Systematic inquiry should be made about the mood and memory of the older person as well as about abnormal behaviour such as wandering and restlessness, irritability, disorientation or night disturbance. Any history of recent physical symptoms or illness must be explored and a note taken of serious past medical history or chronic physical handicap. Many older people misuse or muddle their medication causing mental or physical deterioration so an inventory of current medication taken at home is valuable.

Physical examination
In most circumstances when an older person presents with a psychiatric problem, physical examination by the general practitioner should be arranged. Prior to such examination, the social worker might make an initial appraisal of the person's physical history and state. Inquiries should be made about serious physical illness, hospital treatment or operations and in particular about recent physical changes. Chronic physical disabilities are commonly associated with psychiatric disorders, and the presence of deafness, visual defects, crippling arthritis, chronic heart or chest disease or stroke affecting mobility should be noted. Does the patient look seriously ill? Are they in pain, do they have difficulty breathing or show evidence of an obvious recent weakness or paralysis?

Mental state
Interviewing a mentally ill older person requires skill, patience and often time. The interviewer should aim for a calm, reassuring and confidential approach without interruption, with the older person feeling secure and relaxed.

A clear and formal introduction avoiding any impression of hurry should be followed by careful positioning so that client and interviewer are seated at the same level, close enough to hear without shouting and to make comforting physical contact on hand or wrist if required. The style of the interview should be conversational rather than interrogative and make use of cues in the client's environment or history such as photographs or

work mementoes to convey an interest in the individual. Specific
questions about mood, worries and problems and remembering are
asked within the interview. Psychiatrists usually record the mental state under a series of sub-headings - general behaviour and
appearance, talk, thoughts, mood, abnormal perceptions or beliefs and cognitive state. A social worker should be able to describe the behaviour of the older person at interview, their co-
operativeness, communication and mood. The latter may range
from normal to depressed or suspicious, hypochondriacal, apathetic or irritable, aggressive or agitated. The orientation of
the older person in place, person and time, as well as their concentration and attention, need recording together with an estimate of memory, the latter covering the distinct aspects of
registration, retention and retrieval of information.

Confidentiality and privacy

Anxieties may arise with an older person or other informants
about privacy and confidentiality. Every effort should be taken
to ensure that interviews with the client are not overheard and
similarly that informants have opportunity to express their views
in private. The client or informant must be assured that information given will remain confidential and restricted to the key
professional workers involved such as social worker, team leader
or general practitioner. Clients or relatives may resent inquiries
about their personal lives, finances and background and may
refuse interview, fearing invasion of privacy. Thorough social
and clinical assessment of an older person does involve an invasion of privacy. Where the request for help is initiated by the
older person themselves this can be explained and discussed
directly, but when referral is initiated by others the situation is
more complicated. The social worker must consider whether there
is evidence from the referral request that the older person may
be mentally ill and 'at risk'. If the referral information is inadequate to make a judgment then further inquiry is necessary until
the questions about being 'at risk' and mentally ill can be
answered.

Subsequent investigation should only proceed where significant
hazard, danger or serious mental illness appears evident and
even then only until the essential information for assessment is
gathered, when management decisions are made.

Social assessment

Four major areas should be systematically considered, and a
checklist may be useful for this.

> (i) Living conditions: If the client is living in the community,
> the size of their home, physical condition of the house
> and basic facilities for cooking, heating, washing and
> bathing and layout (e.g. steep stairs) should be docu-
> mented as well as the length of residence and whether it
> is shared.

   (ii) Personal care: How well can the older person cope with dressing, bathing, cooking, shopping, toilet and finances?

  (iii) Dynamics of family/other carers: What are the significant personal relationships of the older person with other family members or key supporters and what are the latter's attitudes and behaviour toward the client? What handicaps or difficulties do the latter have? What was the older person like before they became ill? Does the relative have any time to themselves?

  (iv) Support network: What informal or formal support or assistance does the older person receive from relatives, friends, neighbours or professional agencies? Is district nurse, health visitor or community psychiatric nurse visiting? Are meals on wheels or home help provided? Are the police, solicitors or social security involved?

Medical co-operation

The older client with mental illness will frequently require medical examination as part of a thorough assessment and will occasionally need specialist assessment by a psychiatrist experienced in the psychiatry of old age.

Few field social workers work as integral members of a primary health-care team, and many experience difficulties in communication with GPs concerning action for older clients. In some respects the attitude of many GPs towards social workers has much in common with the response of many older clients, who may show mistrust with the initial social work contact. Doctors, like many other professionals, resent being told what they should do by relatives, patients or social workers. For example, a request phrased, 'You must visit Mrs Jones immediately', is less likely to produce willing co-operation than 'I am most concerned about a serious deterioration in Mrs Jones, whom I saw today, and wondered whether you might be able to help by seeing her as soon as possible?'

Most doctors do not credit social workers with much psychiatric expertise and are likely to feel uneasy if psychiatric jargon or medical diagnoses are used too freely. For example, a request beginning 'Please could you see Mrs Smith who has developed a toxic confusional state probably due to exacerbation of her bronchitis?' is more likely to worry a doctor unfamiliar with a social worker than a request which describes symptoms rather than diagnoses: 'Please could you see Mrs Smith who became abruptly confused yesterday, who has been restless and distressed all night, seeing animals in her flat and no longer recognizes me or her daughter?' In any case a straightforward account of the client's symptoms or complaints in their own words, together with a careful description of their behaviour, based on your own observations or those of a reliable informant, are likely to be of far more value to the GP or psychiatrist in reaching a reliable clinical diagnosis than opinions about or interpretations of symptoms or behaviour alone.

A specialist psychiatric assessment may be required for some clients with complex symptoms or for those for whom specialist facilities such as admission to a psychiatric hospital or a day hospital might be needed. Normal medical protocol dictates that the general practitioner make the request for specialist opinion, which may be for the patient to be seen in the out-patient clinic or in the patient's home as a domiciliary consultation.

Direct requests from social worker to psychiatrist for assessment of a client may be accepted in emergency situations, but on most occasions psychiatrists prefer the GP to have been consulted by the social worker first and to have approved the referral.

The organization and strategy of the specialist psychiatric service for older people shows great variation across the country and social workers should ensure that they understand the strategy of their local service and of the interface with the hospital geriatric services. At present about one-third of the country's health districts have a designated consultant psychiatrist responsible for older people and many of the latter provide a specific liaison service to social services.

It is the policy of the Department of Health and Social Security and Royal College of Psychiatrists for every health district to have at least one consultant psychiatrist responsible for older people, as it is recognized that current provision is often seriously inadequate.

PSYCHIATRIC DIAGNOSIS

An essential part of the assessment of an older person with mental illness is the formulation of the psychiatric diagnosis. It was once thought that specific psychiatric diagnosis was of little relevance with older people because only one disorder - progressive senile dementia - was thought to occur with any frequency. There is now substantial evidence to demonstrate that older people may suffer from a wide range of distinct psychiatric illnesses, most of them with differing prognoses, requiring different treatment and associated with differing hazards and risks.

DEPRESSIVE ILLNESS

Depressive disorders of all grades of severity are common among older people. First, admission rates to psychiatric hospitals rise in middle life to peak in the sixth and seventh decades, and suicide rates begin to increase in the fifth decade and remain high in late life, the rate for men exceeding that for women. A substantial amount of previously unrecognized depressive illness has been demonstrated in screening surveys of older people receiving hospital treatment from medical or geriatric services and among those entering residential homes. Physical ill health increases the likelihood of a depressive illness and so does bereavement and other major personal loss.

The most common form of depressive illness in later life is the agitated depression, which may range from mild neurotic depressive illness to severe psychosis. Almost all sufferers have a hypochondriacal thought content - which may range from fears about autonomic anxiety symptoms, such as palpitations, to bizarre and nihilistic ideas, such as the conviction that their stomach has disappeared. When anxiety is severe the sufferer may make repeated demands for reassurance, to appeal, to importune and to show agitation. Convictions of tremendous guilt may occur. Onset may be abrupt or insidious.

Less common is the depressed person who presents with impaired awareness, self-neglect and memory impairment who may be mistakenly diagnosed as suffering from dementia. In addition, depressive illness may be associated with certain cerebral disorders such as Parkinson's disease and cerebro-vascular disease (the major cause for strokes).

Prognosis and risk in depressive illness
The outcome of depressive illness among older people is variable. Some sufferers, particularly from less severe illness, may recover spontaneously without specific medical treatment often over several months. Even with active psychiatric treatment, which may include the use of anti-depressant medication, admission to hospital as an in-patient or day patient and the use of ECT, about one-third of severely ill sufferers fail to experience substantial improvement. Among those responding well to treatment, at least half are likely to experience a relapse in the succeeding five years. Predictions of outcome by psychiatrists are not highly reliable, but people under the age of 70 generally do better than older patients, as do people with an abrupt onset of severe psychotic symptoms. People with co-existing chronic physical illness, persistent neurotic symptoms or a drinking problem respond less well.

The specific dangers that need to be considered at assessment with depressive illness are:

(i)   Suicide or suicide attempt: Depressed older people are more likely to make successful suicide attempts than younger people, with drug overdose being the most common means. At greater risk are men, people with a drinking problem and those who are single, divorced or separated. The admission of suicidal thoughts or plans in the presence of severe psychotic symptoms with delusions of worthlessness and hopelessness make suicide attempt more likely. Depressed older people who have survived one drug overdose have an increased likelihood of successful suicide with a repeat attempt. Risk of suicide can be reduced with hospital admission, close social support, removal of drugs, development of a confiding pro-

fessional relationship and active treatment of the underlying depressive illness.
(ii) Self-neglect: Neglect of personal hygiene, of nutrition,
of personal and financial affairs and self-care can be a
major hazard with more severely psychotic depressed
older people, particularly for those who also appear confused with a depressive 'pseudo-dementia'. The older
person living alone is most vulnerable. Major improvement is associated with successful treatment of the depression, and the most seriously ill may require hospital
admission, with daily social support often essential for
those remaining at home.
(iii) Relapse or persistence of depression: Relapse of depressive illness with its associated risks of suicide, self-
neglect and suffering is more frequent with increasing
age. Monitoring the mental state and social functioning
of an older person with a history of depressive illness
may prevent relapse or ensure prompt treatment if illness
does recur. Prophylactic drug treatment with anti-
depressant drugs or with lithium requires monitoring and
a careful watch for depressive symptoms or decline in
self-care and will precede medical or social intervention.
In spite of energetic treatment the older person with
persistent depressive symptoms may be severely disabled,
and at risk of becoming over-dependent on friends, relatives or professional agencies. Manipulative behaviour
may alienate the carers and lead to increased isolation.
Because of these factors a marked or severe deterioration
in the depressive illness with risk of suicide may be over-
looked by others.

CONFUSIONAL ILLNESS

Symptoms of confusion may occur in a wide range of disorders,
including depressive illness, and it is particularly important with
a confused older person that a careful clinical assessment including attention to the history is made and a concise diagnosis
attempted. The history from informants should document the onset of the confusion and other mental symptoms, changes in mood,
medication, physical state and social functioning. When it is clear
that the major psychiatric disturbance is confusion, a further
distinction between acute and chronic illness must be made.

Acute confusional illness
This condition is usually short lasting, with a fairly abrupt onset and recovery, and is associated with underlying physical illness. A sub-acute form is also seen in older people where the
onset is similarly abrupt, but followed by a more protracted and
variable course. Clinical features include fluctuations in the level
of awareness and consciousness, and in the severity of all the

associated symptoms which are commonly more severe at night, with brief lucid intervals by day. Memory impairment, distractability and concentration problems together with disorientation and perplexity are additional features.

Visual hallucinations are common in which animals, insects or strangers are seen and illusions and misidentifications are often found, generally associated with fear or panic. Non-specific physical symptoms may include tremor, restlessness and repetitive motor activity, usually coupled with signs or symptoms of the underlying physical illness precipitating the confusion.

Common medical conditions which may cause acute confusion include infections such as pneumonia, heart failure, diabetes, strokes and trauma. Alcohol intoxication or withdrawal, or drug effects from tranquillisers, hypnotics, anti-hypertensive or anti-diabetic drugs or analgesics and many others may precipitate acute confusion.

Prognosis and risks with acute confusional illness
The prognosis of acute confusional illness is essentially that of the underlying physical disorder. Effective medical treatment of remediable disorders such as broncho-pneumonia or heart failure or spontaneous physical improvement following a stroke will usually bring complete mental recovery within days and almost always within a month. Untreatable or irreversible physical illness will often be associated with persistent confusion. Older people who suffer from pre-existing chronic confusion are likely to get worse with physical illness, but if their physical illness is treatable most will return to the level of previous functioning.

The specific dangers or hazards associated with an acute confusional state are:

(i)   Deterioration in physical health and death: An acute confusional state is usually a medical emergency associated with high mortality without clinical diagnosis and treatment. Urgent medical attention will reduce mortality and hospital admission to an acute medical or geriatric ward will commonly be required.

(ii) Disturbed paranoid behaviour: Acutely ill confused older people are often frightened and perplexed and may become suspicious and paranoid and occasionally more disturbed, accusing those close to them, threatening and occasionally assaulting others.

Careful sedation may be required but reassurance from familiar people in familiar well-lit surroundings and avoidance of sudden movement or change are also important. Unfortunately sedation may sometimes increase the confusion or cause loss of consciousness.

(iii) Self-neglect and accidents: The acutely ill and confused older person may fail to eat or drink adequately with consequent dehydration adding to their confusion and physical frailty. Physical unsteadiness and tremor associated

with confusion and lack of judgment increases the risk of
falls or other accidents in the home with the cooker or
fire. Risk avoidance has to be seen in the context of
over-all medical management, but close nursing care at
home or in hospital with supervision of feeding and mobility will substantially reduce these risks.

Chronic confusional illness
This group of chronic conditions are also referred to as chronic
organic psychoses or dementias, with senile dementia and arteriosclerotic or multi-infarct dementia being the most common forms
in older people. They are characterized by multiple and variable
deficits in intellectual functioning, in practical performance and
personality, arising from permanent structural brain damage.
Most start insidiously without an acute phase, but may become
complicated by acute or sub-acute confusion in the presence of
physical illness. Memory impairment is commonly the earliest
deficit often followed by some depressive features with loss of
vitality and initiative. In senile dementia whose time-course from
onset to death ranges to between 3 and 9 years, slowness, repetitive behaviour and gross confusion are usually later features.
Some sufferers have severe speech and communication difficulty,
and other handicaps affecting dressing and the capacity to write
or use ordinary household objects correctly. Between 5 and 10
per cent of people aged 65 and over in the community suffer from
significant chronic confusion and the proportion rises to 25 per
cent of those aged 80 or more.

Prognosis and risk in chronic confusion
The aetiology of senile dementia which is the most common form
of dementia in older people is unknown, and no proven medical
treatment is available to prevent the disorder or arrest or slow
its progress. The specific handicaps, difficulties and impair-
ments in self-care, communication and social functioning vary
quite widely between sufferers, but for all the disorder is associated with substantially increased mortality with a mean life
expectancy from onset to death of about five years.
   The specific hazards or dangers which may need review at the
assessment conference on a chronically confused older person
are as follows:

(i) Self-neglect: For the older person with dementia living
    alone neglect of personal hygiene, feeding and finances
    will frequently be significant hazards. The older person
    may not remember to wash properly, to change under-
    wear or to do washing and may be unable to follow through
    plans for food purchase, preparation and consumption on
    a regular basis. It may be possible to reduce these
    hazards by setting up specific domiciliary services or
    providing day care or, more radically, by admission to
    hospital or residential care. Weekly district-nurse visits

to attend to personal hygiene, laundry service and meals on wheels perhaps coupled with home-help service may reduce these hazards substantially provided the older person is co-operative. Relatives, neighbours or social worker may need to assume responsibility for monitoring or handling finances, and, if the latter are substantial or complicated, legal mechanisms such as power of attorney for the mildly confused or court of protection for the more disabled client may need to be enacted.

(ii)   Safety and accidents at home: Accidents in the home are more common with confused older people than those who are alert, but the risk is not evenly distributed. The older person who is both physically frail or unsteady on his feet as well as being confused is more likely to have a fall than the more robust, and the danger is further increased if the older person is restless and disorientated at home.

Physical aids such as rails on stairs, toilet or bathroom and the provision of safer seating at appropriate height as well as safety gates and fire-guards may help to reduce this risk. The fear of accidents with cooker and fire because of forgetting to light the gas or failure to smell a burned pan is frequently one of the strongest anxieties among relatives or neighbours. In practice, domestic gas explosions are extremely rare and it is uncommon for confused older people to burn themselves or cause a serious fire. An assessment of an older person's safety with domestic appliances and fires can be made in their own home by an occupational therapist employed by hospital or local authority, and it will often be possible to reduce the hazard by, for example, turning the gas off at the mains while the family are at work with an old person alone in the house, replacing cooker or fire for one with an automatic pilot-light and installing central or night-storage heaters to replace open fires where finances permit and the older person co-operates.

(iii) Wandering and road-traffic accidents: Only a minority of chronically confused older people are both physically fit enough and energetic enough to present serious problems because of wandering away from home, and even then it is rarely a regular and persistent behaviour. For some older people restless wandering behaviour is associated with physical illness or with environmental change or may only occur at certain times of the day or night. A confused older person may become lost wandering away from home, but only a minority of wanderers present a serious hazard to traffic. Assessment of the dangers must include a careful description of the chronology and precipitating factors. A variety of strategies may reduce the risks. Where the timing of the wandering is predictable, day care or sedation in the evening or night may prevent it.

Simple security precautions such as double-locks for the front door may prevent wandering while the weary spouse is in the garden or resting. Identification on clothing or handbag of the older person will expedite return home and the local police may be of additional help.

(iv) Physical illness: The chronically confused older person is more likely than others of the same age to suffer from physical illness, and as a consequence of their confusion they or their relatives may fail to recognize the symptoms of physical illness and neglect or forget to seek medical attention. In addition the confused older person living alone may be erratic and unreliable with essential medication.

Relatives and others monitoring the older person's functioning need to keep an eye on their physical condition and mobilize medical assistance with significant change. Clear labelling and setting out of medication perhaps on a daily basis with removal of other drugs and simplification of drug regime will also reduce risk.

(v) Health and safety of carers: The caring environment for a confused person living with family is rarely emotionally stable for long. The spouse, daughter or other relative will undergo an evolving emotional response, which may range from mild anxiety to severe depression, from anger to denial. Relatives may find it difficult to accept the radical change in the personality and behaviour of the confused person and may become ill themselves with a depressive illness or become so frustrated or tormented that they may walk out on the older person. Some demented older people become more irritable or aggressive towards their relatives and where this occurs there is sometimes serious risk of physical harm to them or to their relatives since self-control may be lost by either party. Several strategies may reduce this risk. Supportive casework for the carers in which their guilt, anger or depression can be acknowledged and reduced may help as well as practical advice from a community psychiatric nurse on ways of handling the irritable, confused older person. Day care may be life-saving for the carers who may need time to themselves, and careful monitoring of the mental state of the carers is essential.

(vi) Loss of freedom: The confused older person is only too often deprived of freedom and independence. Discussion and decisions about the problems and placement are often undertaken by relatives and professionals with the older person excluded, and the opinion of the latter given little weight. Although great efforts have been made to improve the quality of care in most residential homes and long-stay hospitals for older people in the past decade, most older people with confusion become institutionalized very quickly and few homes or hospitals have staffing levels

or regimes which actively encourage independence for
their confused residents. Relatives of an older person at
home, nurses and residential care workers are more likely
to feel anxious about the older person's safety than their
independence. Mention was made, in the preceding chapter, of Norman's discussion document on rights in old age
and this can again be recommended in this context (Norman, 1979).

PARANOID ILLNESS

Paranoid symptoms are fairly common among older people and may
occur in a variety of conditions and circumstances. Some people
with sensitive or paranoid personalities habitually feel hostile or
suspicious. In addition, paranoid interpretations often occur
when perception or awareness is impaired, as with deafness,
acute organic confusional states or dementia. Paranoid beliefs
become fragmented and less coherent as confusion becomes more
severe. Severe persecutory or grandiose delusions (fixed abnormal beliefs) may also be seen in depressive illness. Generally
distinct from these conditions is the functional paranoid illness
of late life (also known as paraphrenia) which commonly runs a
chronic course untreated and is often associated with auditory
hallucinations, elaborate paranoid beliefs and remarkably normal
mood. There is a wide range of severity and many sufferers are
deaf, socially isolated or have long-standing paranoid personality
traits.

Prognosis and risks in paranoid illness
The prognosis for paranoid symptoms in older people is essentially the prognosis for the specific underlying disorder. An
older person who has always been sensitive and mistrustful will
usually remain so and may resent or resist assistance from caring
agencies, even when specific hazards such as physical ill health
are drawn to their attention. The confused paranoid person may
threaten or assault carers in his confusion because of misiden-
tification and may benefit from reassurance, a non-confronting
approach with distraction or diversion to other topics or activities
a valuable tool. Careful sedation with a phenothiazine such as
thioridazine may also be helpful. The use of phenothiazines for
the treatment of functional paranoid illness of late life (paraphrenia) in the past two decades has transformed its prognosis.
Complete or substantial symptomatic improvement occurs in most
more severely ill patients, although continued paranoid attitudes
may persist. It may be difficult or impossible to negotiate a treatment contract with a very paranoid individual and compulsory
admission to psychiatric hospital under the Mental Health Act may
need to be considered occasionally where the risk of starvation or
serious threat to the safety of others is present. In general,
workers with paranoid older people must accept that close or

trusting relationships are rarely possible and casework is often more effective using a contractual model than a confiding psychotherapeutic one.

EMERGENCY AND CRISIS MANAGEMENT

Mental illness in older people often develops insidiously, as does most dementing illness which causes chronic confusion and as do many depressive illnesses. In contrast, presentation of a mental illness problem to health or social services for the first time is commonly as a crisis. The social-work department and health professionals at primary care and specialist levels need a strategy and structure for dealing with emergencies but specific management plans are likely to be more effective if the aetiology of the crisis is analysed first.

Crisis aetiology
Crisis among older people with mental illness may be precipitated for a variety of reasons, sometimes multiple. The older person may have become physically unwell due to an infection, stroke or many other physical causes. As a consequence, behaviour may deteriorate abruptly with the development of an acute confusional illness and physical symptoms are also likely to be present. On the other hand, the physical or emotional environment of the older person may have changed, with consequent acute confusion or distress or depression in the vulnerable subject. Examples of physical change are moving house, admission to hospital or residential care. Equally traumatic for other fragile older people may be the death of a spouse or the absence of key supporter on holiday or the stress of emotional conflict or interpersonal dispute at home. In other situations the tolerance of the carers towards a confused older person may be abruptly exceeded even though the older person's behaviour may not have recently changed, and the carers may suddenly demand assistance or total release from their responsibilities.

The caring system may be manipulated by anxious relatives or carers and a crisis engineered for a range of different reasons. Where local services for older people with confusion are inadequate, with poor collaboration between services, and GP, psychiatrist and social worker reluctant to take responsibility for providing support and care, an emergency may be fabricated in order to get some action. For example, a family may call a relief service doctor out of hours, claiming in desperation that an acute physical problem has just arisen where the regular GP has been unresponsive.

A general practitioner may attempt to obtain an acute medical hospital admission for an older person pleading a recent stroke, where psychiatrists or geriatricians operate with a vast waiting list. Confused older people requiring residential care may be prematurely discharged home from hospital in an attempt to

force the provision of emergency residential care where hospital
staff feel thwarted by lengthy waiting-lists and pressure on
their acute beds.

A crisis may also be caused in care settings unfamiliar, ill-
equipped or antagonistic to older people with mental symptoms.
For example, a surgical or medical ward may panic and press
for 'disposal' of a recently admitted older person with some
symptoms of confusion without any serious attempt to obtain an
informed history or assess the patient fully. Similarly, panic or
anxiety may arise among residential care staff when confusion
presents in a recently admitted resident. General practitioners,
social-service duty-desk staff and psychogeriatricians are
familiar with the Monday-morning crisis, often consisting of
daughter or son urging immediate action from health or social
services following their weekend visit to the elderly relatives
and subsequent anxiety or guilt about their condition. A
different version may be present on Friday afternoon when relatives or other carers become anxious about reduced support at
weekends and urge hospital or residential care admission to
prevent disaster although the behaviour and functioning of the
older person may have been stable all week.

Crisis management
A crisis requires prompt assessment and appraisal, and a swift
decision in the first instance about whether a genuine medical,
psychiatric or social emergency exists. Urgent referral to
medical or psychiatric services will be required for medical or
psychiatric emergencies, and social workers doing emergency
work should be informed of local protocol and guidelines for
emergency referrals and the overlaps and gaps between these
services. The emergency provision of shelter for the protection
of relatives or an older person from aggression or violence may
require emergency social intervention. Professionals called in
emergency or crisis are usually under substantial pressure to
act promptly and urgently, often with admission to care, and
considerable courage may be required to resist these pressures
and formulate realistic management plans based on proper assessment.

Klaus Bergmann (1978) has used flowcharts to clarify some of
the options in diagnosis and management in a psychogeriatric
crisis. His intitial stem question begins 'Is the patient intellectu-
ally impaired and/or has he a clouded sensorium' and for an
affirmative answer is followed by a question about recent impairment.

If impairment is recent, systemic illness may be the cause,
and a subsequent decision made about diagnosis and management
at home. If hospital admission is required in these circumstances,
medical, surgical or geriatric admission is usually more appropriate than psychiatric. Where the intellectual impairment is of
longer duration, senile or arteriosclerotic dementia are the most
likely causes and if recent physical illness is not a complication

then the crucial question is 'Can relatives and/or friends cope?'.
Where the carers are prepared to cope symptomatic treatment
coupled with social support and supervision will be required. If
unable to cope the succeeding question is 'Is behaviour disturbance or wandering the main problem?'. When it is a major problem psychiatric admission will need to be considered and if not
local authority residential care or geriatric hospital care may be
more appropriate.

Bergmann's discussion reflects the nationally accepted view of
the British Geriatrics Society, Royal College of Psychiatrists and
Department of Health that the institutional care of the older
person with dementia should be determined by the presence or
absence of significant physical illness or disability and presence
or absence of disturbed behaviour, with the three continuing
care settings - geriatric wards, psychiatric hospital and residential homes each providing a home for substantial numbers of
chronically confused older people.

In his analysis of a psychogeriatric crisis without intellectual
impairment Bergmann's three key questions are 'Are depression,
guilt, sleep disturbance and loss of energy prominent features?',
'Has the patient delusions and/or hallucinations?' and 'Has there
been a recent change in health and/or social or family circumstances?' with psychiatric opinion essential when the answers to
the first two are affirmative and social support often essential
when the answer to the third question is yes.

LONGER-TERM MANAGEMENT

Risk analysis

The starting-point for risk analysis is comprehensive assessment,
which will include liaison with other professionals already involved with the client. Fresh opinions may be sought from psychiatrists, geriatricians or general practitioners where preliminary
social work assessment suggests the need for clinical appraisal.
Assessment of self-care functioning by an occupational therapist
in the client's home or nursing assessment by a district nurse
will be relevant for some referrals. The opinion and appraisal by
the client of their own situation and difficulties is often over-
looked or ignored, but needs recognition and consideration
alongside the other professional views.

The hazards to which an older person with mental illness is
exposed frequently change with time and the needs for social
work, medical or nursing services in order to avoid risks will
vary. It is particularly important to establish good interprofessional relationships and communication because of these
changing needs and to avoid the client falling between stools due
to over rigid definitions of agency responsibility.

The material collected in the assessment process then needs to
be carefully analysed by the professional workers involved with
the client. Where the client has been referred to the specialist

psychiatric service, the analysis and review will usually take
place at the multidisciplinary ward round held weekly and
attended by team social worker or area social worker by special
invitation. Area social workers must consider whether to set up
a case conference using a risk analysis chart to assess the
dangers. Case conferences can facilitate communication and the
allocation of responsibility between workers, but busy professionals are not always free to attend. Where a formal case
conference is impracticable or inappropriate the onus remains
with the social worker to liaise with the other professionals and
identify the hazards, dangers and strengths in the client's
situation.

According to Brearley (1980) the risk analysis framework is a
structure for the organization of knowledge for action in specific
situations, and specification of hazards, dangers and strengths
in a particular case should be followed by agreement on hazard
management.

Hazard management
A first step for the workers involved having identified the
hazards is to decide which of the hazards needs to be tackled
first and, then, how to remove, avoid or lessen the hazard.
Deciding which of several hazards deserves priority may be a
difficult task requiring predictive and manipulative skills for
the workers involved. In many cases hazard avoidance will involve several workers, often from different disciplines and a
positive multidisciplinary approach will make it much easier to
allocate the specific tasks and responsibilities to the different
workers involved. The term multidisciplinary approach is
preferred to the notion of a multidisciplinary team because the
notion of consistent multidisciplinary team applies primarily to
hospital specialist teams, whereas with the majority of area
referrals the different workers involved do not consistently
work together as a close team, but only share a common purpose
in relation to the specific referral.

Key worker and task sharing
Task sharing between disciplines maintains a wider perspective
on the needs of the older person and may also help to lessen
anxieties of the workers involved. It will sometimes be appropriate to designate a key worker, but open communication and
anxiety sharing should not be restricted. Responsibility sharing
provides a degree of insurance for the workers involved and may
reduce stress.

Agreement to designate a key worker does not mean that the
others involved can opt out of their responsibilities to the client,
although the key worker will carry responsibility for the co-
ordination of appropriate services to meet the client's needs.

All workers with the elderly mentally ill should be aware of the
speed with which the problems and needs of the older person
may change, requiring reassessment and often new referral to

additional agencies, as, for example, when a chronically depressed widow supported by both home help and a social worker develops a chest infection and needs urgent medical attention. Monitoring the changing needs and hazards to which the older person is exposed is a vital task which may be performed by either the key worker or someone in regular contact, such as volunteers, home help or district nurse.

Resource allocation – the social-work task
Following assessment and risk analysis the main social-work task becomes one of allocating appropriate resources so that the risks and hazards to which the older person is exposed are reduced to an acceptable level. The multidisciplinary case conference will often be the most useful forum for defining an acceptable level of risk, the process sometimes reducing the stress felt by individual workers.

The allocated social worker with an older mentally ill client must acquire an extensive knowledge of the resources available in that district or area which may be used to avoid or reduce the hazards to which their client may be exposed. Some of these resources will be provided by the local authority, others by voluntary or private agencies or by the health service. The level and quality of provision of services such as day care, social and luncheon clubs, meals on wheels, home help, sheltered housing and short and long stay residential care varies from area to area as does the health-service provision. What is needed above all is a creative and imaginative approach in which the person at risk is offered services which are tailored as far as possible to meet their individual needs.

Care needs to be taken to define aims and objectives when new services are provided to meet the needs of the older person or some of their supporters, coupled with recognition that the need for specific services is likely to change with time. Ongoing assessment and monitoring of a situation should be built in. For some clients the major social-work task will be referral to appropriate support services, but for many ongoing social-work involvement will be essential. Here again, careful consideration must be given to clarify the tasks the worker will be expected to carry out. The social worker's role may be a very active one where casework skills are used to help to change interpersonal attitudes within the family or to modify the response of the older person to outside help or change. The social worker may in addition provide support to older people and their families, thereby helping to maintain them in their own homes. Family members caring for a confused or mentally ill older person may need opportunities to discuss their problems and occasional or regular breaks from caring. Sometimes the major social-work task for a period of time with the client may simply be regular monitoring, and consideration should be given to using alternative workers such as a neighbour, home help or volunteer for this role. Before closing a case or delegating monitoring responsibility to someone else, an effort must be made to weigh up the possible difficulty for the older person of establishing a new relationship and to describe the often subtle behavioural changes that may be warning signs of crisis and often best appreciated in the context of a relationship extending over time

Example 1 : Depression Mrs S is a 75-year-old widow living alone without close friends or acquaintances. She was depressed almost continuously after her husband's death two years earlier and had two overdose admissions to hospital, but showed substantial improvement with a brief psychiatric admission. She returned home and attended a day centre twice weekly but developed worrying physical symptoms associated with anxiety which her GP was investigating. She has two married sons with their own families in regular contact, but living at a distance, who were anxious about a further overdose and were pressing for residential placement. Assessment information was available from psychiatrist, occupational therapist, nursing staff, team social worker, general practitioner, day-centre manager and from Mrs S and her son. Table 5.1 identifies the general hazards, situational hazards, dangers and strengths of the situation.

Soon after her return from hospital, it was agreed that the most serious danger was a further overdose, and that her loneliness and isolation were the situational hazards requiring most urgent action to reduce the risk of depression and further overdose. The social worker planned to work directly with Mrs S on this problem, but in close co-operation with the day-centre manager to increase the frequency of her attendance there and with the volunteer bureau who introduced Mrs S to a neighbourhood volunteer.

Example 2: Chronic confusion Mr B is a 72-year-old retired bus-conductor who lives in a ground-floor council flat with his second wife to whom he has been married for seven years. She has a past history of depressive illness. Her first husband died from cancer ten years ago and she nursed him during his final illness. In recent months Mrs B has experienced difficulty in coping with the change in Mr B's behaviour, particularly his persistent questioning and increasing dependence, and because of this her GP requested a visit from the psychogeriatrician. Mr B was diagnosed as suffering from senile dementia although it was in the early stages. However, it was felt that there were certain hazards present in the situation because of Mrs B's past history and the situation was discussed by the psychogeriatrician, the social services, the GP and the day-centre manager (see Table 5.2)

It was apparent that Mrs B's only support system in caring for her husband came from a daughter from her first marriage and that she resented the lack of support from her husband's family. It was agreed that the following supports should be offered:

Table 5.1 Depression

	Predictive hazards	Situational hazards	Strengths	Dangers
Mrs S	Age. Widowed. Poor physical health. Depressive illness.	Isolation/lack of support. Distance from sons. Inability to cope with upkeep of flat. Depression. Refusal of extra support.	Son's concern. Day-centre attendance. Social-work involvement.	Loneliness. Another overdose. Lack of attention. Admission to residential care.
Sons	Conflict between needs of mother and own family.	Increasing needs of mother. Distance from mother. Anxiety about another overdose.	Good relationship with mother.	Marital stress. Guilt if mother should overdose again. Death of mother.
Social worker	Lack of resources.			Admission of Mrs S to residential care.

(a) Day care three times weekly for Mr B at a centre for the elderly confused.
(b) Relatives support group for Mrs B.
(c) Individual social casework and support for Mrs B.
(d) Occasional relief admissions to residential care for Mr B.

These supports were successfully implemented but after six months a crisis occurred. Mrs B decided to take Mr B on a short holiday to a boarding house with her and this was very unsuccessful because of his socially unacceptable behaviour which embarrassed her greatly.

On her return home she contacted the day-centre manager threatening to walk out on her husband. The manager listened to Mrs B at length and offered a prompt further interview which averted the serious danger of her desertion and then contacted the social worker. As a result Mr B has now been promised a regular respite admission to residential care every six weeks which enables his wife to continue caring for him at a level with which she can cope.

Example 3 : Chronic confusion   Mrs C is a 72-year-old widow who was living alone in a three-bedroomed, semi-detached house in a quiet residential area prior to her hospital admission. She retired from her clerical job with London Transport five years ago and her husband died soon after. They had no children and her only relative is her husband's sister who lives about eighty miles away.

Mrs C is a pleasant friendly lady who is well liked by her neighbours but became an increasing source of anxiety to them after her husband's death. She spent little time in her home and it became very dirty with cupboards full of food. She often knocked on her neighbours' doors at inappropriate times and was found wandering in the street. She was also found trying to light a fire with a can of paraffin. Her neighbours contacted the social services department but Mrs C turned down all offers of help from the social worker who visited.

However, her physical condition worsened suddenly and she had to be admitted to hospital where she was found to be suffering from a chest infection, a urinary-tract infection and toxic confusion as well as malnutrition. With treatment her physical health improved but it became apparent that she was chronically confused and disorientated with a poor short-term memory.

Mrs C was taken on a home visit by the occupational therapist and a ward nurse in order to help decide future options for her. It became clear from this that she had extreme difficulty in carrying out the minimum tasks which would be necessary for her to live at home again.

At this point the hospital team social worker was involved and an analysis was made of Mrs C's situation by the multidisciplinary team using information from Mrs C's neighbours and GP as well as the knowledge gained during her hospital stay. The social

Table 5.2 Chronic Confusion

	Predictive hazards	Situational hazards	Strengths	Dangers
Mr B	Dementing illness. Second marriage.	Disorientation. Inability to communicate. Persistent pestering behaviour.	Day-care attendance. Affection for wife.	Wife's tolerance – may give up care.
Mrs B	History of depressive illness.	Depression. Mr B's persistent pestering behaviour.	Social-work support. Relatives' support group. Daughter's support.	Guilt if unable to care for husband.
Social worker				Inappropriate admission of Mr B to residential care.

Table 5.3   Chronic Confusion

	Predictive hazards	Situational hazards	Strengths	Dangers
Mrs C	Age. Widow. Dementing illness. Few relatives.	Isolation. Fire/forgetfulness. Cooker/forgetfulness. Growing confusion. Failure to eat.	Helpful neighbours.	Social withdrawal. Lack of attention to her wishes. Malnutrition. Untreated physical illness.
Sister-in-law	Age. Widow.	Distance from Mrs C.		
Neighbours	Age.		Professional support.	Fire caused by Mrs C.
Social worker		Pressures from neighbours.	Multidisciplinary support.	Mrs C's inappropriate admission to care. Mrs C's death.

worker also talked with Mrs C so that she could contribute to
plans for her future.

It was thought by the professionals that the dangers involved
in Mrs C's return home were unacceptably high and a decision
was made to try to place her in residential care. Mrs C was taken
for a preliminary visit to a residential home and was very willing
to have a trial stay there. She was transferred from hospital
and settled well. Her financial affairs were referred to the Court
of Protection because of her inability to deal with them but she
was informed about this and fully accepted the rearrangement.

6 RISK AND HEALTH CARE

Michael Hall

Many changes occur in the human body with age which affect its function. These occur either as a result of age or disease processes. The incidence of illness increases with age and with it disability, so that much of the functional deterioration may be so attributable. These changes, whether as a result of age or illness, represent hazards which may put individuals at risk. It is the objective of this chapter to consider how these health or ageing hazards create risk, and how these risks may be minimized so that the individual can lead an active life, maintaining a role in society as well as developing his own individuality by exploring new concepts and gaining new experience.

The concept of hazard and risk in relation to health is an interesting one and may vary in relation to the time and sequence in which they occur. Potential for risk resulting from hazard may relate to the immediate and the long term, for example, dental extraction represents a hazard which can give rise to the immediate risk of an abnormal reaction or allergy to the anaesthetic which may be given as part of the extraction procedure. Alternatively, tooth fragments could be inhaled and so represent an immediate risk arising from a need for dental extraction. Inhalation of a tooth fragment is itself a hazard which gives rise to immediate or long-term risks. There might be the immediate risk of hospitalization with further instrumentation such as bronchoscopy, itself a hazard with its own risks; or if inhalation of fragments was not recognized at once, the longer term risk of lung infection or even lung abscess with possible long-term risks of chronic lung disease. Consequently the concept of hazard and risk when applied to health care has a sequential nature of causes and outcomes and if viewed in this way can help the social worker or the non-medical professional to understand many of the health problems posed by the older person. Prevention of hazard will obviously reduce risk and many hazards may be prevented by relatively simple methods, such as environmental adjustment.

'FAILURE TO THRIVE'

Perhaps the commonest symptom of which many old people complain is what in children is often termed a 'failure to thrive'. Older people attribute this symptom to 'old age' and this explanation is frequently taken at its face value by carers whether

they are relatives, neighbours or even professionals. The symptom therefore represents a hazard and creates the danger of the
older person being labelled as disabled or unable by the caring
agency. Once this has happened the situation is difficult to reverse since subjects will rapidly accept disability as attributable
to age and therefore irreversible so that they label themselves
as unable. As a result of this disuse, residual abilities are neglected and atrophy. This has been described elsewhere as the
negative health cycle (Figure 6.1), which is much easier to prevent than to correct. Consequently, an accurate diagnosis of
the 'failure to thrive' is essential if optimum function of those
labelled as 'able' is to be maintained.

'Failure to thrive' may be defined as a 'performance' problem.
In other words, the individual feels that his function is no longer
normal and his ability to do things is diminished. A reason for
this will exist. To discover this we must, like the small child,
ask the question 'Why?'. The answer will only be found by making a full assessment of the individual's capability. To do this
his total state of health, in its widest sense, must be considered
and the triple assessment of his physical, mental and social state
made.

This may seem a daunting task for anyone to undertake, but
if the functional deficit is viewed in performance terms then
pointers to a solution may be easily found. Mager and Pipe (1970)
have suggested that analysis of any performance problem will
demonstrate one of two basic causes: the individual lacks either

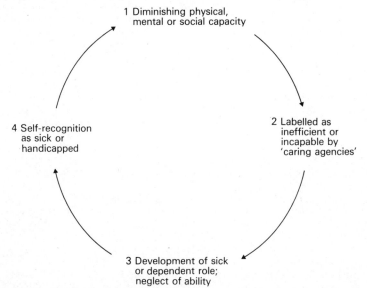

1 Diminishing physical,
mental or social capacity

2 Labelled as
inefficient or
incapable by
'caring agencies'

3 Development of sick
or dependent role;
neglect of ability

4 Self-recognition
as sick or
handicapped

Figure 6.1 The negative health cycle: a vicious circle of ill
health in the elderly

skill or motivation. Translating this into health care terms,
one needs to ascertain if the lack of 'skill' or ability results
from a physical disability which in turn has an underlying
cause. If this cause can be corrected then the disability will
disappear and the 'skill' of the individual to perform appropriately will return.

A simple example is to consider the house-bound state. This
may result from a 'failure to thrive', in other words, failure to
thrive represents the hazard, the danger of which is becoming
house-bound. This in turn could lead to isolation which in turn
could lead to loneliness, loneliness to depression, depression to
suicide, etc. The prevention of the house-bound state could
therefore be a matter of some importance. The disability, however, may result from the fact that the individual is so breathless on exertion that he is unable to walk more than a few steps
and consequently unable to walk out of his house and into the
street. His impaired performance and therefore his lack of 'skill'
or ability, is a direct consequence of his breathlessness. If his
breathlessness can be abolished, then his exercise tolerance
should automatically improve, and his house-bound state will disappear. That hazard with all its consequent hazards will thereby
be removed. Correction of his breathlessness, therefore, is the
prime objective since the removal of this hazard will remove its
consequent risks. If the breathlessness is due to illness, its correction may be possible as a result of accurate clinical diagnosis
and treatment. On the other hand, disease processes may have
caused irreversible lung changes which cannot be remedied or,
in the very aged, the breathlessness may result from age changes
in the lung. Nevertheless, even in these cases, it may be possible, by physical training methods, by environmental readjustment, or the provision of the appropriate aids, to alter performance so that the house-bound state no longer exists. For instance,
if physical-training techniques fail to produce an improvement in
performance, mobility itself may be improved by the provision of
a self-propelled or mechanically propelled chair. Alternatively,
environmental adjustment such as rehousing may be equally
effective if, for instance, he lives on the side of a hill, the slope
of which represents a difficulty which he cannot overcome. Re-
housed on the flat, walking without discomfort might be possible.
Similar situations can arise for people who live in flats without
lifts.

Symptoms such as breathlessness may also reduce the individual's motivation to remain active for they may be sufficiently
unpleasant to be regarded as a state of punishment. Leaving the
house means walking either up or down hill: if walking up hill
causes 'punishing' discomfort then the only option is to go down
hill, yet to do so means the house can only be regained with distress. Such 'punishment' may be unacceptable, so the option is
rejected and motivation to go out is lost. Similar rejection of an
option will occur among older people who suffer from depressive
illness or other mental or physical disease which causes discom-

fort of sufficient level to make the effort to overcome the discomfort unrewarding.

Viewing the symptoms of disabilities of the elderly as 'performance' problems may make their elucidation and solution by the
investigating professional easier since it is possible to construct
a simple flow chart for each problem (Figure 6.2). It must, of
course, be understood that such a sequence will only be initiated
if the functional discrepancy is sufficiently important to justify
the steps which will need to be taken. Finally, having defined
the problem the best solutions must be selected and implemented.
These won't necessarily be medical.

Assessment is, therefore, of great importance. Simple obser-
vation of, for instance, the individual's appearance can often
indicate a good deal. Attention should be paid to colour or text-
ure of their skin. Anaemia or jaundice are both conditions which
will give rise to malaise. Weight loss may be apparent and may
indicate some underlying organic condition which may or may not
be remediable. Alternatively, it may indicate sub-nutrition resulting from loss of appetite which in turn may have many causes.
The individual's appearance may also presage his mood: somebody
who is neat and well-kempt and groomed is unlikely to be depressed. The individual's energy or lethargy may be apparent and
their intellect may be obviously impaired. Their hearing or vision
may also be deteriorating. As already indicated, mobility may be
of great importance. It may be limited, not only by breathlessness as has been suggested, but also by diseases of the joints or
lack of appropriate foot care. Equally a small bladder syndrome
may limit an individual's ability to go shopping and in consequence lead to a house-bound state. Swollen ankles may often
be a sign of immobility or even heart failure. Sleep disturbance
and habit may also be clues to other abnormalities. Medicines
and drugs may often give rise to undesired effects (adverse reactions) or even interact inappropriately with one another. Two
sedatives, for instance, given together may sometimes produce
less sedation rather than more.

It can be seen from this that the symptom 'failure to thrive'
represents a risk which may result from a whole series of hazards which in turn may be preventable. Other symptoms when
elucidated may be the root cause of this syndrome; it is perhaps
logical to consider these as hazards which, in turn, may represent risks arising from other hazards. The type of flow pattern
that follows is shown in Figure 6.3.

Symptoms should not necessarily be considered as either 'Hazards' or 'Risks'. Swollen ankles, for example, may not be hazardous in themselves, if nothing is done about them and they are
unassociated with other symptoms. They will only become a hazard if they are considered of sufficient importance to warrant
drug treatment which then becomes hazardous. They will only
become risky if they result from heart failure or venous obstruction. Nevertheless, symptoms are often signposts to hazards
and risks since they represent the discomfort of which the patient

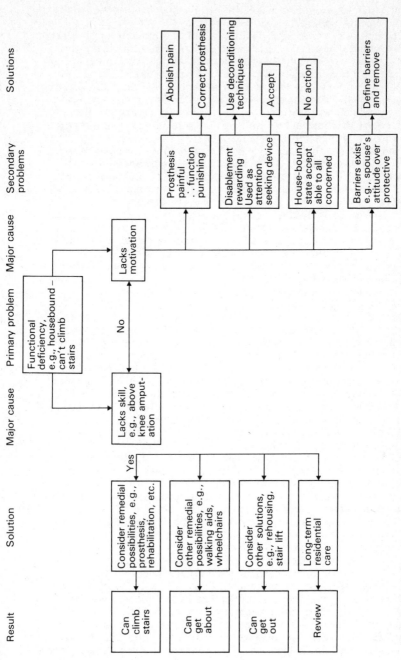

Figure 6.2 Flow chart to show how problems (hazards) may be analysed

complains. In considering health-care hazards and risks a symptomatic approach is probably the easiest.

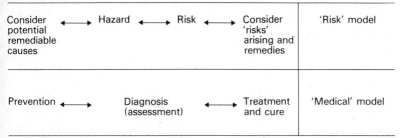

Figure 6.3   Flow diagram comparing the 'risk' model with the conventional 'medical illness' model

CARDIORESPIRATORY SYMPTOMS

Introduction
The heart, lungs, arteries and veins comprise the cardiorespiratory system. Basically, the heart consists of two muscular pumps, each having an inlet and outlet valve and connected to one another by the systemic and pulmonary blood vessels. The lungs drain into the left heart which then pumps the oxygenated blood through the arteries to supply all the organs, muscles and tissues of the body. Disease or ageing processes may affect any part of the system. In order to work efficiently the heart requires competent valves and a healthy muscle. The muscle or any of the valves may be affected by disease or ageing processes. Since they are subjected to greater pressure, the left-sided heart valves are more likely to become diseased or affected by age changes. Similarly, since it has more work to do, the left-sided heart muscle may be more prone to failure. If this happens the blood received from the right heart cannot be removed by the left and consequently the lungs become congested. This means that the lungs become wet, the patient complains of breathlessness and coughs up frothy and sometimes blood-stained sputum. Following this the right heart frequently fails and the venous side of the body becomes congested so that the liver becomes engorged, enlarged and painful and the ankles swell, becoming oedematous.

Heart-muscle failure is frequently associated with poor blood supply to the heart muscle itself by the coronary arteries. This may be associated with blockage of the coronary arteries, i.e. coronary thrombosis and consequent myocardial infarction. This is commonly associated with a crushing type of chest pain. It may also occur when the heart muscle gets starved of blood, the pain being known as angina pectoris. The circulation through the body, i.e. the systemic circulation, is maintained by the heart rate and by the stroke volume, the product of the two being the cardiac output. This is about five litres a minute in health. Blood pressure depends on the resistance within the blood vessels to the flow of blood and both heart rate and resistance may be controlled by impulses generating from the autonomic nervous system.

Heart failure
It can be seen, therefore, that the symptoms associated with heart failure may be those of breathlessness, enlargement of the liver, abdominal pain and tenderness, ankle swelling, cough, frothy sputum and chest pain. All these symptoms may give rise to sufficient discomfort to limit the individual's ability to perform those acts which are necessary for his normal daily life and be made worse by exertion. Moreover, the blood circulating through the body will be inadequately oxygenated and consequently the organs and tissues of the body will not receive appropriate nourishment to function properly. This may affect brain function as well as other organ function so that toxic substances may accumulate and waste products not be eliminated. This hazard may produce mental confusion, a hazard in itself, which will carry its own risks.

Vascular insufficiency (ischaemia)
Shortage of blood to the brain and other organs may result from the inability of the impulses in the autonomic nervous system to maintain an adequate pressure within the vessel walls. As a result, blood pressure may fall in association with standing or exercise so that inadequate circulation is maintained to the brain. This can cause the symptom of fainting and falling. The subject may momentarily lose consciousness and such a hazard causes the risk of trauma, particularly that of a fracture of the lower limb bones. Similar organ ischaemia (lack of blood) will result if the arteries are narrowed by disease processes such as arteriosclerosis, if this occurs in the peripheral arteries of the legs, the subject may complain of pain in the calf when walking – a symptom known as intermittent claudication since the pain resolves when the walking stops. The symptom will reduce activity and may produce isolation and loneliness. If the blood vessel, however, becomes occluded by the disease process or by blood clot, then the tissue supplied by that blood vessel will die. If this happens in the leg, then gangrene will ensue. In this case the hazard will produce the danger of amputation. Alternatively, if it happens in the brain, then a stroke and paralysis may ensue.

Abnormal heart rhythms (arrhythmias)
Similar vascular occlusion or insufficiency may result from abnormal heart rhythms. These may produce insufficiency due to the inefficient pumping action of the heart or as a result of blood clot forming in the heart and then being dispersed to other parts of the body (i.e. embolism). Abnormal heart rhythms therefore present a hazard which may be associated with the risk of faint-

ing episodes, falls, strokes or gangrene. The recognition of such a hazard is obviously of great importance since to prevent it occurring may remove a whole series of dangers. Such abnormal rhythms may sometimes be diagnosed by monitoring the heart's rhythm over a period of twenty-four hours using a portable tape-recorder connected to an electrocardiographic lead. This may enable the arrhythmia to be diagnosed and corrected, perhaps by insertion of an electrical pace-maker which will regularize the heart's action. Alternatively, it may be possible to abolish the abnormal rhythm using a drug.

Lung disease
Good lung function is essential for good gaseous exchange to occur. Obviously, therefore, any disease of the lung will affect this gaseous exchange and reduce the amount of oxygen which is available to the organs and tissues of the body. Lung disease will be associated with the symptoms of breathlessness, cough and the production of sputum which may sometimes be copious, contain pus and be bloodstained. Subjects with acute lung diseases particularly those who suffer inflammatory lung diseases such as pneumonia or get acute pulmonary emboli are usually acutely ill. Chronic inflammatory lung disease is often associated with chronic obstructive airways disease, and wheezing is less debilitating and some subjects may be able to lead relatively normal lives if acute exacerbations of their illness can be avoided. This may, however, require permanent drug therapy and medical supervision. Pulmonary tuberculosis may run an insidious course in old age and present the individual with relatively little disability apart from cough and a little sputum. Nevertheless, the hazard is ever present and the risk involves the infection of children and young adults. Chest X-rays are, therefore, of importance in older people and should be done whenever an individual fails to thrive. Finally, the symptom of cough or breathlessness may indicate an underlying cancer of the bronchus or lung, which may or may not be amenable to treatment. This obviously carries the risk of many complications but these too may be amenable to the appropriate treatment.

NEUROLOGICAL SYMPTOMS

Senile dementia (organic brain syndrome, chronic brain failure)
Intellectual impairment probably represents a major symptom and therefore hazard. Disorientation of the individual in time and space, associated with loss of higher intellectual function, constitutes a diagnosis of dementia. This may have various causes and reversal of the basic brain damage is usually impossible. Nevertheless, the individual's condition may still be adequately managed and performance improved by appropriate therapy. The hazard of senile dementia carries a risk of unacceptable abnormal behaviour. Carers may find this difficult to tolerate without the

support of a good community psychogeriatric service. All subjects with intellectual impairment must be fully and adequately assessed so that a firm accurate diagnosis can be made. While senile dementia is a common cause, depressive illness can sometimes present as a dementing process or may complicate a mild dementia making it much worse. Alleviation of depression may therefore remove a hazard and reduce the risk of unacceptable behaviour. Acute confusional states may also persist if their cause is not treated and brain failure may be associated with hypothyroidism, pernicious anaemia or normal pressure hydrocephalus.

Depressive illness
Depressive illness itself is common in old age as are other psychiatric disorders such as neurosis and paraphrenia. Although depression is a hazard in itself, it frequently occurs as a result of physical illness causing diminished function and the inability to lead a useful life. Removal of those hazards relating to physical illness will, therefore, do much to alleviate the depression itself and thereby reduce the risks which the hazards of drug treatment may provoke.

Stroke illness
Stroke illness is common in old age and the incidence of stroke after the age of 75 is probably about 8/1000 population per annum. Stroke, as has already been mentioned in the cardiorespiratory section, results from the blockage of a cerebral artery usually as a result of thrombosis or a combination of embolism and thrombosis. It has been shown to be associated with a high blood pressure and it is possible that the prevention of hypertension at a young age may reduce the incidence of stroke illness in old age. 'Strokes' vary in their severity. Some are associated with severe coma and consequently death, others are transient, symptoms clearing within twenty-four hours. These latter, often called transient ischaemic attacks, may themselves carry the risk of stroke at a later date. Prevention of this may be possible by drug therapy which reduces the risk of blood clotting. These drugs themselves represent hazards with their own risks. Trials are currently being conducted but as yet no clear evidence of benefit exists.

In most people's mind, paralysis of one or more limbs, plus or minus the loss of speech, is the common result of a stroke. Such an occurrence represents a considerable hazard since mobility will be limited and the individual may become dependent on the help of others for continuing existence. Rehabilitation following a stroke needs to be intensive and is probably best carried out in special units where staff are trained to cope with the problems which these patients present.

Sensory deprivation
(a) Hearing Sensory abnormalities are common in association with

ageing and the sensory deprivation syndrome is well recognized.
Degeneration of the outer hair cells of the organ of corti causes
high tone hearing loss at a comparatively early age. Exposure
to excessive noise (hazard) may accelerate this degeneration and
worsen it but the hearing impairment of old age or presbyacusis
is almost universal. Hearing loss, however, has to be quite
marked before hearing is sufficiently impaired to make a hearing-
aid necessary. Nevertheless, its effects are often underestimated
for the subject is still able to hear, though clarity of discrimination is lost (hazard). This often represents an embarrassment
to the individual who tries to hide his disability by guessing at
what has been said. If the 'cues' and 'clues' have been misinter-
preted, his guess may often be wildly wrong and his hearing
impairment misdiagnosed as mental confusion. Because of their
inability to make contact with other people's lives, older people
who are hard of hearing may often be incorrectly labelled. Moreover, because of their self-consciousness, they frequently become isolated and may also become excessively suspicious,
hallucinate and develop psychiatric illness which may be either
depressive or paraphrenic in type (see also, Chapter 5).

(b) Vision Age changes occur in the lens and in the eye at a
relatively early age and few people will not have suffered the
effects of presbyopia by the time they are 50. However, because
most people are frightened of going blind, visual symptoms are
usually reported relatively early to doctors. Although blindness
does occur in old age, most visual disturbances are amenable to
treatment and can be improved. Blindness associated with diseases of the eye in old age is comparatively uncommon and
usually results from occlusion of the retinal artery or detachment of the retina itself. Conditions such as temporal arteritis,
which may be associated with occlusion of the retinal artery,
must therefore be diagnosed early and treated since blindness
can then be prevented if this is done. Similarly, retinal detach-
ments can be halted or even repaired if treated early enough.
Obviously, though, the visual impairment, like hearing impairment, is a hazard with obvious consequential dangers. Social
isolation and depressive illness are common and environmental
adjustment to provide good lighting, together with additional
social activities, can do much to alleviate the symptoms and
reduce the risk.

Taste and smell
Other sensory abnormalities include the reduction of smell and
taste and these are almost universally diminished after the age
of 80 years. As smell and taste are closely interlinked they
represent hazards which lead to the danger of sub-nutrition.
Moreover, the inability to smell may represent its own risk with
relation to gas leaks.

Other sensory abnormality
Skin sensation is often difficult to assess in old age but some
people may complain specifically of a cotton-wool feeling in the
soles of their feet when walking. This is a symptom of neurological disease and may be linked to diabetes mellitus or pernicious
anaemia or other forms of peripheral neuropathy. Both these
conditions are treatable and although the sensory abnormality
may not be much improved its worsening may be preventable.

Dizziness
Other common symptoms involving the neurological system are
tremor, dizziness and falls. Dizziness may frequently be associated with hearing impairment and may be associated with an
ageing or disease process affecting the labyrinth and the organs
of balance. It may sometimes be associated with circulation abnormalities affecting the brain stem, or degenerative changes
occurring in the joints of the neck. It represents a hazard with
the danger of falling and its consequential effects. It may be
extremely difficult to manage and alleviate from a medical point
of view. Appropriate environmental adjustment, such as making
blankets more accessible in case of a 'long lie', may be the
most effective method of management (see below).

Tremor
Tremor is frequently asociated with Parkinson's disease but may
occur without known cause in old age. It obviously makes movement, dressing and feeding more difficult and may, in fact, lead
to nutritional deficiencies. Resulting unsteadiness may also lead
to falls and if, as is frequently the case, it is associated with
increased muscular rigidity, ability to rise following a fall may
be severely limited.

Falls
Falls are common among older people. Many occur as a result of
true accidents such as trips, missing a step or slipping. Others,
however, occur as a result of cardiorespiratory disease, neurological disease or diseases of the skeletal system which may limit
mobility, joint movements and the ability to balance effectively.
Any symptom which represents a hazard with the risk of falling
is serious. Moreover, falls themselves represent a hazard, one
danger of which may be a 'long lie' in an exposed position until
someone comes to pick the individual up. The 'long lie' has
recently been shown to be in itself a hazard which is associated
with an increased likelihood of death. The assessment of a patient
who is liable to fall is therefore of paramount importance. In the
first instance, all possible causes of falls must be eliminated and
treated. If, however, it is not possible to prevent the fall, then
the individual should be taught what to do about it when he has
fallen. If he cannot be taught to get himself up off the ground
(and referral to the day hospital with this specific purpose in
mind may be of great value) adjustment of the environment and

appropriate social organization must be undertaken. Appropriate
alarm systems may be of great value but they must be devised
so that they are accessible to the patient. Some form of regular
social contact must be arranged even if it is only via the telephone. Appropriate heating and lighting systems must be in-
stalled so that the individual can remain warm even though he
has fallen. Blankets and pillows should be kept at an accessible
level so that they can be used by the individual while he waits
for help and so reduce the risk of hypothermia.

SKELETAL SYSTEM

Joint disorders

Diseases of the skeletal system, i.e. those that affect the bones,
joints and muscles, will tend to limit the mobility of the patient
and therefore his ability to get out and about and lead a normal
life. Diseases of bones, joints and muscles are often interlinked,
in as much as joint disease may lead to muscle atrophy and bone
thinning: these latter two conditions being the result of disease.
Symptoms of swelling and pain associated with joint disease (arthritis) therefore carry the risk of both bone and muscle atrophy.
The resulting muscle weakness will, in itself, represent a hazard,
limiting mobility, and the loss of power may make it more difficult
for the individual to maintain his balance and make him more
likely to fall. If he falls then his thinner bones may be more
likely to fracture. The hazards and risks involved are plain to
see. The alleviation of pain, prevention of joint deformity and the
maintenance of mobility are therefore of prime importance if the
dangers of skeletal disease and deformity are to be diminished.
A large pharmacological armamentarium exists for the control of
pain due to arthritis. Unfortunately, almost all the drugs used
for this have their own potential hazard and risk phenomenon.
Particularly at risk is the gastrointestinal system which may bleed
as a direct result of the action of some analgesic drugs such as
aspirin and other non-steroidal anti-inflammatory drugs. Alternatively, constipation, a hazard with its own sequence of risks
and hazards (see below), may result from the individual's reduced
mobility, poor diet, and drug therapy, particularly if morphine
analogues are used as analgesics.

Considerable progress has, however, been made in recent years
with regard to the surgical replacement of joints that have become severely diseased. Hip replacement in particular has been
extremely successful and other joints such as elbows and knees
may also be replaced.

Bone disorders

Bones may also become diseased as a result of the ageing process
or as a result of metabolic diseases. Often the two conditions,
osteoporosis and osteomalacia, may occur together in old age.

While osteoporosis may be part and parcel of the ageing process, it is much more common in women and there would seem to be an undoubted endocrine link in association with the menopause. It is likely that some women lose calcium in excessive amounts at this time of life and consequently their bone mass is depleted. The hazard of osteoporosis therefore may be amenable to appropriate therapy and this risk may in time be eliminated. Osteoporosis has been defined as a condition in which there is too little bone, though what bone there is is normal. Such bones are particularly at risk in subjects who fall and in severe cases even the act of standing up may be sufficient to cause a fracture.

Osteomalacia may frequently be associated with diseases of the gastrointestinal tract. This may result in vitamin D deficiency and the condition can be reversed by appropriate treatment. Vitamin D deficiency may also be a risk of a poor diet which is deficient in the vitamin: those who experience long-term illness or severe disability are particularly exposed to this danger. It is also well known that vitamin D metabolism in the body is dependent on exposure to ultraviolet light (sunlight) and consequently production may be diminished in the house-bound who never get into the sun. Exposure to ultraviolet light will correct this deficiency. Vitamin D deficiency is also associated with a proximal muscle weakness (myopathy). This particularly affects the thighs and means people can't get up from a chair, climb stairs, etc., except with difficulty and help. Mobility will be limited. Yet this hazard and its consequences can easily be reversed.

Paget's disease of the bone is another bone condition common in old age. It is associated with over-production of bone so that the bone becomes deformed. It may cause pain and immobility, lead to fractures and even be associated, when very advanced, with high output heart failure. Drug treatment for the condition is now available.

Finally, the bone is a common site of primary and secondary cancer. This may lead to pathological fracture. It is often presaged by bone pain which can be relieved by X-ray therapy. Fractures may be prevented by appropriate pinning or plating of the bone before the fracture occurs and over-all prognosis may be quite good.

ALIMENTARY SYSTEM

Loss of appetite

Loss of appetite (anorexia) is a common symptom among older people. It represents a danger which may be the result of a variety of hazards. It is commonly associated with lesions of the gastrointestinal system, particularly local lesions of the mouth, which may make mastication of food uncomfortable, or disorders of the digestion, which may be associated with nausea, indigestion or even difficulty in swallowing. It may be associated with mental illness such as depression. It may also be associated with neurological disorders particularly those which may interfere with the sensation of taste and smell and it has already been mentioned that these may be lost as part of the ageing process. Loss of appetite may also occur as a result of other diseases which make the ingestion of food difficult, e.g. Parkinson's disease, so that the individual gets into the habit of eating less and consequently wanting less. Loss of appetite invariably leads to dietary deficiency and consequently subnutrition. This may be associated with vitamin and mineral deficiencies which may present in a variety of ways. Iron deficiency, for instance, is a common cause of anaemia, a hazard which can lead to the danger of heart failure. Since a poor dietary intake is so common in association with illness in older people, its likelihood should always be considered in all individuals who have hazards which are likely to produce this risk. Consequently all frail and disabled older people ought to receive vitamin supplements.

Dysphagia (difficulty in swallowing)
Ingestion of food may become limited by anything which makes swallowing uncomfortable or difficult. A sore mouth is not an uncommon symptom in older people and, although this is not a true cause of dysphagia, it may very well limit dietary intake. It may itself be a result of vitamin deficiency but may also be associated with aphthous ulceration or sore gums which may be associated with badly fitting dentures or even allergy to the plastic material of which the dentures are made. Dysphagia itself may be associated with lesions of the oesophagus and abnormal muscular contractions associated with the ageing process are not uncommon. The condition is sometimes called presbyoesophagus. Narrowed segments, strictures which may be either benign or malignant, may also be associated with the symptom of dysphagia and these may particularly follow peptic ulceration in association with hiatus hernia. Most of these conditions are treatable but an accurate diagnosis needs to be made in order to assess the condition properly.

Vomiting
Vomiting is a common gastrointestinal symptom in old age. It may, or may not, be associated with nausea. It usually indicates a gastric lesion that may be associated with hiatus hernia particularly when this is associated with free regurgitation of food and stomach contents. Vomiting may also be associated with disorders of balance such as vertigo and also occur with vascular lesions which affect the vertebro-basilar system and particularly the cerebellar arteries themselves. Vomiting may also be associated with gastrointestinal infections and also obstructive lesions of the outlet of the stomach (pyloric stenosis) which may be malignant. An accurate diagnosis of the cause of vomiting is always essential. The hazard can lead to deficient dietary intake as well as a considerable loss of fluid and consequently dehydration.

Abdominal pain
Abdominal pain is a frequent symptom of alimentary tract disease
and is often associated with the symptoms of vomiting and anorexia. Pain is often associated with peptic ulceration and in this
case is usually associated with food, being either relieved by its
intake or provoked depending on the site of the ulcer. Other
lesions associated with pain are usually the result of obstruction
of the gastrointestinal tract and are usually colicky in nature and
may be associated with neoplasms. Ischaemic bowel disease is not
uncommon. It may also be associated with acute abdominal pain.
Inflammatory lesions of the abdomen are frequently painless and
common conditions such as acute appendicitis, empyema of the
gall bladder, diverticulitis, may occur silently. Their presenting
features may be those of confusion and general malaise and even
quite severe peritonitis may be relatively painless. A high degree
of suspicion is often necessary to make an accurate diagnosis of
these conditions which carry a bad prognosis.

Constipation
Because older people tend to be immobile, reduce their dietary
and fluid intake and often eat a low residue type of diet, constipation can be a common and troublesome symptom. It is often
aggravated by drugs which are given to treat other conditions.
For instance, diuretics may produce dehydration and anticholin-
ergics will tend to reduce gut motility. Analgesics, particularly
if these are morphine derivatives, may also be contributory. The
risk, therefore, of constipation in older people is high and is the
result of many hazards. It is itself a hazard which can lead to
mental confusion. It may, moreover, present as diarrhoea and be
associated with faecal soiling and incontinence. This hazard may
lead to the patient being regarded as socially unacceptable and
make carers resistant to the individual's return home. Fortun-
ately, the condition often leads to hospital admission though this
is a hazard in itself which may result in the individual picking up
hospital infections. However, once in hospital, constipation is
usually easily treated and appropriate adjustments can be made
in the management of the patient's care to prevent its recurrence.
Moreover, once carers are aware of its likelihood, prevention is
usually possible.

GENITO-URINARY SYSTEM

Urinary incontinence
Like faecal incontinence, the hazard of urinary incontinence tends
to make individuals socially unacceptable to care in the community.
The symptom is often looked upon as a disgraceful one by the individuals themselves as well as their carers and its occurrence
may often be concealed. This is a pity as a great deal can be done
to improve incontinence. While it would be incorrect to suggest
that all cases can be treated successfully, a great many can be

markedly improved. An accurate diagnosis of the cause of incontinence is absolutely essential and investigation in hospital
may be necessary to achieve this. Once an accurate diagnosis of
the cause has been made then various lines of treatment are possible. These may involve drug therapy, surgical treatment or
toileting management regimes which may lead to the individual
regaining complete control of micturition. If this is not possible,
then it may be possible to minimize the effects of the incontinence by the use of the appropriate appliances and in some patients, catheterization may prove acceptable and abolish the
condition. It is true, therefore, to say that in almost all cases a
solution can be found to the problem of urinary incontinence and
the hazard removed. However, some forms of treatment may represent hazards with their own consequential risks.

DISEASES OF THE ENDOCRINE GLANDS

Diabetes mellitus
Maturity onset diabetes is common among older people. However,
by no means all patients who suffer from this condition require
treatment with either insulin or other hypoglycaemic drugs. Individuals with this condition may well present with thirst and
polyuria and also present with a 'failure to thrive' syndrome and
lethargy. The condition can often be controlled by dietary measures alone. This may, however, mean that the individual has to
stick to a specialized diet and this may be difficult for him or her
to provide.

Thyroid disease
Both hypothyroidism and hyperthyroidism are relatively common
occurrences among older people. The diagnosis of hypothyroidism
may be particularly difficult as many of its clinical features mimic
those of the ageing process itself. Consequently subjects with
this condition gradually slow down performance and become more
constipated and gradually become less active. Treatment with replacement therapy can reverse the condtiion. An early diagnosis
is particularly important if irreversible mental deterioration is to
be prevented.
   Hyperthyroidism or thyrotoxicosis is also fairly common and
often difficult to spot as the patient may sometimes be apathetic
rather than excited. All individuals, however, with heart failure
or cardiac arrhythmias should be suspected of having hyperthyroidism and appropriate tests carried out. Therapy, again, is
easy since the thyroid gland can be damped down with small doses
of radioactive iodine.

Other endocrine diseases
All the other endocrine diseases which occur in younger patients
can also occur in old age, and some, for instance, hyperpara-
thyroidism, may be commoner than is generally realized. Some of

these conditions are often associated with alterations in intellectual performance and consequently they should be suspected
whenever abnormal behaviour in the older person is encountered
They may also present in association with bone disease and general metabolic disturbances and with general decline in ability.
A diagnosis is frequently not easy. This applies to many conditions from which older people suffer.

CANCER

The incidence of cancer rises with age and some cancers may be
particularly common. For instance, it is estimated that a quarter
of men over the age of 90 have cancer of the prostate. This, however, does not mean that all these patients need treating since
the cancer will often only be discovered after microscopic examination performed after death, having given no symptoms in life.
The course of many cancers in older people may be relatively
benign and may very often be controlled with appropriate chemo-
therapy. In many others, the cancer may be an incidental finding
which may neither limit activity nor shorten life. Consequently
accurate diagnosis of cancer is important and appropriate treatment should always be instituted. Moreover, when cancer is likely
to prove a terminal event and cause death, accurate diagnosis
can make patient management more positive and pain relief more
certain.

DRUG THERAPY

It should be considered that all drugs represent hazards with
their own consequential dangers. Because the incidence of disease rises with age, it is likely that many older people will have
to take drugs in order to maintain their function and performance.
As can be seen from the foregoing paragraphs, drugs will be
needed to treat many conditions. For instance, digitalis and
diuretics may be needed to treat heart failure, hypnotics to manage sleeplessness, tranquillizers to manage anxiety, antidepres-
sants to relieve depression and analgesics to relieve pain. All
these substances are potential hazards and many physicians in
geriatric medicine tend towards therapeutic nihilism, because
they see so many patients get better when the drugs which have
been poisoning their systems are stopped. It has, for instance,
been suggested that 70 per cent of the people who are taking
digitalis for heart disease don't really need it. When one knows
that digitalis can give rise to anorexia, nausea, vomiting, visual
disturbance as well as almost every cardiac arrhythmia which has
been described, one can see how potent a medicine it is. Nevertheless, its use may be vital to the survival of some individuals
as active, intelligent and happy people. We have to accept, therefore, that drugs are going to be essential to the management of

illness in many older patients. They should be used wisely and
their use constantly monitored to ensure that they are still necessary and still proving effective.

CONCLUSION

The foregoing has been a brief account of some of the problems
which arise in the health care of older people. Geriatric medicine
is a comparatively new speciality and the specialist in this medical discipline has been trained to study the diseases of the
elderly. One hundred years ago the famous French physician
Jean Marie Charcot wrote that a knowledge of senile pathology
was essential to the management of illness in older people. Illnesses in older people are hazards which produce dangers. Frequently these are themselves hazards which produce further
risks. Accurate assessment and diagnosis of every hazard,
whether it be physical, mental or social, is essential if that hazard is to be eliminated and the risk of diminished performance,
whether this be physical, mental or social, eliminated.

Health care of older people is a rewarding field in which to
work. Even when cure is not possible, much can be done to reduce risk and improve quality of life by enabling people to be
happier and more active.

7 CONCLUDING

'A widespread misconception is that problems in old age are rarely of an urgent nature. The reverse is true, since everything to do with old people needs to be regarded as requiring utmost speed' (Williamson, 1978, p. 41). The need for help among older people tends to arise either from the clustering or collection of various hazards in the life of someone living alone, or as the result of a breakdown in the supporting network of family, friends and services. Sometimes such breakdown is the result of accumulated family strain but more often it is a combination of such strain and an unexpected or sudden family emergency. Whatever the cause, if services are required they may often be needed in a hurry. Problems are not exclusively urgent and the previous chapters have set out to explore some of the different time dimensions in work with older people.

One issue which this book has attempted to deal with is the need to present ageing and 'being older' as normal experiences encountered by everyone, while at the same time recognizing that many older people do find old age a time of problems. There has therefore been a dual underlying objective. First, to present the information, ideas and theories which are available to understand the phenomena of ageing and of old age in order to provide a perspective from which to view problems, needs and risks. Second, to identify specific hazards and deficiencies in the lives of older people which make them vulnerable as a group and which, for a substantial minority, create imminent and serious danger. The dilemma which is encountered in social work with older people is the need to recognize the importance of encouraging and maintaining a process of ageing in a profession which is primarily problem orientated. One way of overcoming this dilemma which has been offered here has been the recognition of the relationship between need and risk. Deficiencies in the present represent hazards for the future and decisions can only be made by, with and for older people, if the dangers are clarified. Only if it is clear what could happen, how likely each possibility is and how attractive or undesirable each outcome is can priorities be organized. Need and risk are therefore central and interlinked aspects of practice with older people.

This inevitably involves a recognition of the importance of a concept of taking risks as well as of the passive identification and management of vulnerability or 'at riskness'. The law relating to the care of older people is often vague and imprecise. The National Assistance Act, for instance, uses the terms 'care and attention', the Health Service and Public Health Act speaks of promoting the welfare of the elderly and other government papers refer to 'support', 'care', and 'attention'. The result is that the social worker's duty to protect older people is unclear. Although in some ways this increases the opportunity to be flexible in providing care, it increases the pressure on the individual worker whose vulnerability to criticism may be heightened. Work with the elderly lacks clear decision rules and this has major significance for risk management. Some priority guides exist in some local authority departments but they tend to be general in nature. The British Association of Social Workers' 'Guidelines for Social Work with the Elderly' (1977) offers useful, but again very general guidelines. Clear decision rules can provide:

1 An outline of the best available practice and knowledge to serve as a model to strive for.
2 A basis for social worker and social-work agency self-protection: if decisions are made according to established practice there is a measure of justification and freedom from blame if loss occurs.

While such an approach does carry the dangers of limiting initiative, flexibility and desirable risk taking, it seems essential to strive for greater precision and understanding of good practice guides in this field of work.

In order to make older people and those who work with them safer a number of elements seem particularly important:

1 Establishing standards of good practice in specific contexts, and, therefore,
2 Establishing criteria and guidelines for action.
3 Providing regulations and procedures within agencies: including goal planning and reviews, supervision and efficient management of staff and resources.
4 Establishing a safe environment for workers and for older people – but recognizing that total security is neither possible nor desirable.
5 Increasing knowledge and research in the field. Considerable strides have been made in recent years but our level of knowledge about older people and ageing is still preliminary when compared to the field of child care.
6 Development of education and training. The wider dissemination of knowledge and changes in attitudes are essential to the development of this field of work.

Finally, these comments should be related back to the exploration of risk analysis in the Introduction and in the Introductory book of this series (Brearley, 1982). Good risk management and good practice depends, with any group, on thorough analysis and purposeful planning. This is no less true of older people than of any other age group.

BIBLIOGRAPHY

Abrams, M. (1977a), 'Profiles of the Elderly: Aspects of Life Satisfaction', vol. 3, Age Concern, England.
Abrams, M. (1977b), 'Profiles of the Elderly: Who are they?', vol. 1, Age Concern, England.
Abrams, M. (1978), 'Beyond Three Score and Ten', Age Concern, England.
Abrams, M. (1980), 'Beyond Three Score and Ten: A Second report on a Survey of the Elderly', Age Concern, England.
Abrams, P. (1977), Community care: some research problems and priorities, 'Policy and Politics', vol. 6, p. 125.
Agate, J. (1972), 'Geriatrics for Nurses and Social Workers', Heinemann.
Age Concern, England (1974), 'The attitudes of the retired and the elderly'.
Age Concern, England (1978), '"A Happier Old Age": A Response to the Government Discussion Document'.
Age Concern, Greater London (1980), 'Discharge from Hospital: The Social Workers' View'.
Arie, T. (1971), Morale and planning of psychogeriatric services, 'British Medical Journal', vol. 3, pp. 166-70.
Association of County Councils (1979), 'All Our Future'.
Baltes, P.B. (1973), Strategies for psychological intervention in old age: a symposium, 'The Gerontologist', vol. 13, no. 1, spring 1973, pp. 4-6.
Barley, M. and Wilson, J. (1979), Boarding out officer helps the old, 'Community Care', 11 October, pp. 28-9.
Beardon, W.O., Mason, B.J. and Smith, E.M. (1979), Perceived risk and elderly perceptions of generic drug prescribing, 'The Gerontologist', vol. 19, no. 2, pp. 191-5.
Beaver, M.L. (1979), The decision-making process and its relationship to relocation and adjustment in old people, 'The Gerontologist', vol. 19, no. 6, pp. 567-74.
Bebbington, A.C. (1978), 'The Elderly at Home Survey: Changes in the Provision of Domiciliary Social Services to the Elderly over Fourteen Years', University of Kent Personal Social Services Research Unit, discussion paper no. 87.
Bell, B.D. (1978), Disaster impact and response: overcoming the thousand natural shocks, 'The Gerontologist', vol. 18, no. 6, pp. 531-40.
Bengston, V. (1973), 'The Social Psychology of Aging', Bobbs-Merrill.
Bergmann, K. (1978), Psychogeriatrics, in Carver, V. and Liddiard, P. (eds), 'An Ageing Population', Open University.
Beth Johnson Foundation and the Beth Johnson Housing Association (1978), 'Responses to the DHSS Document: "A Happier Old Age"'.
Blaire, T. (1978), Self-help and the elderly: a summary of the working group discussions, in Glendenning, F. (ed.), 'Self-Help and the Over-60s', Beth Johnson Foundation/University of Keele.
Blau, Z.S. (1973), 'Old Age in a Changing Society', New Viewpoints, Franklin Watts.
Blenkner, M. (1966), 'Environmental change and the ageing individual', Proceedings of the Seventh International Congress of Gerontology, Vienna.
Blenkner, M., Bloom, M. and Nielson, M. (1971), A research and demonstation project of protective services, 'Social Casework', vol. 52, no. 8, pp. 483-99.
Blunden, R. and Kushlick, A. (1974), 'Research and the Care of Elderly People', Wessex Health Care Evaluation Research Team, Research Report no. 110.
Bosanquet, N. (1978), 'A Future for Old Age', Temple Smith/New Society.
Boswell, D.M. (1969), Personal crisis and the mobilization of the social network, in Mitchell, J.C., 'Social Networks in Urban Situations', Manchester University Press.
Botwinick, J. (1966), Cautiousness in advanced age, 'Journal of Gerontology', vol. 21, pp. 347-55.
Botwinick, J. (1969), Disinclination to venture responses vs cautiousness in responding age differences, 'Journal of Genetic Psychology', vol. 115, pp. 55-62.
Bowder, B. (1980), 'Ageing in the '80s', Age Concern, England.
Bradshaw, J., Clifton, M. and Kennedy, J. (1978), 'Found Dead: A study of Old People found Dead', Age Concern, England.
Brearley, C.P. (1975a), 'Social Work, Ageing and Society', Routledge & Kegan Paul.
Brearley, C.P. (ed.) (1975b), 'Self-Help, Participation and the Elderly', University of Southampton.

earley, C.P. (1976), Social gerontology and social work, 'British Journal of Social Work', vol. 6, no. 4, pp. 433-47.

earley, C.P. (1978), Ageing and social work, in Hobman, D. (ed.), 'The Social Challenge of Ageing', Croom Helm.

earley, C.P., Gibbons, J., Miles, A., Topliss, E. and Woods, G. (1978), 'The Social Context of Health Care', Blackwell/Robertson.

earley, C.P. (1980), Welfare goals, in Dickson, N. (ed.), 'Living in the 1980s', Age Concern, England.

earley, C.P. et al. (1980), 'Admission to Residential Care', Tavistock Publications.

earley, C.P. (1982), 'Risk in Social Work', Routledge & Kegan Paul.

earley, C.P. and Richardson, J. (1975), Social work in a geriatric hospital, 'Social Work Today', vol. 6, no. 8, 10 July, pp. 229-32.

itish Association of Social Workers (1977), 'Guidelines for Social Work with the Elderly'.

ocklehurst, J.C. (1978), Ageing and health, in Hobman, D. (ed.), 'The Social Challenge of Ageing', Croom Helm.

ocklehurst, J.C. et al. (1978), Medical screening of old people accepted for residential care, 'The Lancet', no. 8081, 15 July.

omley, D.B. (1974), 'The Psychology of Human Ageing', Penguin.

ooks, D. (1977), Social workers have not helped in care in general practice, 'Update', June, pp. 1395-8.

ubaker, T.H. and Powers, E.A. (1976), The stereotype of 'old': a review and alternative approach, 'Journal of Gerontology', vol. 31, no. 4, pp. 441-7.

uckingham, G., Dimmock, B. and Truscott, D. (1979), 'Beyond Tea, Bingo and Condescension', Beth Johnson Foundation/Task Force.

utler, A.W.J., Oldman, C.M. and Wright, R.M.A. (1979), 'Sheltered Housing for the Elderly: A Critical Review', University of Leeds, Dept of Social Policy and Administration, Research Monograph.

utler, R.N. (1960), Intensive psychotherapy for the hospitalized aged, 'Geriatrics', vol. 15, September, pp. 644-58.

utler, R.N. (1963), The life review: an interpretation of reminiscence in the aged, 'Psychiatry: Journal for the Study of Interpersonal Processes', vol. 26, no. 1, February, pp. 65-76.

utler, R.N. (1975), 'Why Survive? Being Old in America', Harper & Row.

amden, London Borough of (1978), 'Joint Assessment of the Elderly: The first 6 months', Social Services Dept.

amden, London Borough of (1979), 'Joint Assessment of the Elderly', vol. 2, Social Services Dept.

arter, K. and Evans, T.N. (1978), Intentions and Achievements in Admissions of the Elderly to Residential Care', Clearing House for Local Authority Social Services Research, no. 9, University of Birmingham.

artwright, A., Hockey, L. and Anderson, J.L. (1973), 'Life Before Death', Routledge & Kegan Paul.

hallis, D. and Davies, B. (1980), A new approach to community care for the elderly, 'British Journal of Social Work', vol. 10, pp. 1-18.

hambers, R. (1980), 'Personal responsibility in old age', in Dickson, N. (ed.), 'Living in the '80s', Age Concern, England.

hapman, P. (1979), 'Unmet Needs and the Delivery of Care', Occasional Papers on Social Administration, no. 61, Bedford Square Press.

hown, S.M. (1972), 'Human Ageing', Penguin.

igno, K. (1979), Where do they all come from?, 'Community Care', 18 January, pp. 26-7.

larke, R. (1980), Volunteers: the basic questions, 'Community Care', 10 April, pp. 18-19.

oleman, P. (1979), Health expectations are the key to well-being in old age, 'Modern Geriatrics', vol. 9, no. 3, pp. 57-8.

oni, N., Davison, W. and Webster, S. (1980), 'Lecture Notes on Geriatrics', 2nd edn, Blackwell.

ontinuing Care Project (1980), 'Organizing Aftercare', NCCOP.

ook, F.L., Skogan, W.G., Cook, T.D. and Antunes, G.E. (1978), Criminal victimization of the elderly: the physical and economic consequences, 'The Gerontologist', vol. 18, no. 4, pp. 338-49.

ooper, J.D. (1980), 'Social Groupwork with Elderly People in Hospital', Beth Johnson Foundation.

orrigan, P. and Leonard, P. (1978), 'Social Work Practice Under Capitalism: A Marxist Approach', Macmillan.

oventry Social Services (1972), 'Looking for Trouble Among the Elderly'.

rawford, M. (1972), Retirement and role-playing, 'Sociology', vol. 5, no. 1., pp. 217-36.

Cresswell, R. (1977), Social networks, 'Community Care', 26 January.
Cumming, E. and Henry, W.E. (1961), 'Growing Old - The Process of Disengagement', Basic Books.
Darvill, G. (1980), 'Crossing of Purposes', the Volunteer Centre.
Davies, E.M. (1975), 'Let's Get Moving', Age Concern, England.
De Alarcon, J.G. (1971), Social causes and social consequences of mental illness in old age, in Kay, D.W.K. and Walk, A. (eds), 'Recent Developments in Psychogeriatrics' Royal Medico-Psychological Association.
DHSS (1976), Some aspects of residential care, 'Social Work Service', no. 10, July, pp. 3-17.
DHSS/ Welsh Office (1978), 'A Happier Old Age', HMSO.
Disability Alliance (1979), 'The Government's Failure to Plan for Disablement in Old Age
Dowd, J.J. (1975), Aging and exchange: a preface to theory, 'Journal of Gerontology', vol. 30, no. 5, pp. 584-934.
Dowd, J.J. (1980), Exchange roles and old people, 'Journal of Gerontology', vol. 35, no. 4, July, pp. 596-602.
Dunham, A., Nusberg, C. and Sengupta, S.B. (1978), 'Toward Planning for the Aging in Local Communities: An International Perspective', International Federation on Ageing.
Dunphy, R. and Lodge, B. (1979), Promoting natural living in a residential home for elderly people, in MIND, 'Choosing How to Live'.
Elder, G. (1977), 'The Alienated: Growing Old Today', Writers & Readers Publishing Co-operative.
Erikson, E.H. (1964), 'Childhood and Society', revised edn, Norton.
Ferlie, E. (1980), 'Directory of Initiatives in the Community Care of the Elderly', University of Kent, Personal Social Services Research Unit.
Finkel, S. and Fillmore, W. (1971), Experiences with an older adult group at a private psychiatric hospital, 'Journal of Geriatric Psychiatry', vol. 4, pp. 188-99.
Freeman, J.T. (1980), 'Aging: Its History and Literature', Human Sciences Press.
Freeman, M.D.A. (1979), 'Violence in the Home', Saxon House.
Friedsam, H.T. (1962), Older persons in disaster, in Baker, G.W. and Chapman, D.U. (eds), 'Man and Society in Disaster', Basic Books.
Fry, M. (1954), 'Old Age Looks at Itself', Churchill Livingston.
Gibberd, K. (1977), 'Home for Life: Residential Care: What Alternatives?', Age Concern England.
Gilhome, K. (1974), Emotional needs, in 'The Place of the Retired and the Elderly in Modern Society', Age Concern, England.
Gilmore, A. (1976), Old people's pets keep loneliness at bay, 'Modern Geriatrics', vol. 7, no. 43.
Glendenning, F. (ed.) (1978), 'Self-Help and the Over-60s', Beth Johnson Foundation/ University of Keele.
Goldberg, E.M., Mortimer, A. and Williams, B.T. (1970), 'Helping the Aged', Allen & Unwin.
Goldberg, E.M. and Warburton, R.W. (1979), 'Ends and Means in Social Work', Allen & Unwin.
Goldberg, E.M., Warburton, R.W., McGuiness, B. and Rowlands, J.H. (1977), Toward accountability in social work: one year's intake to an area office, 'British Journal of Social Work', vol. 7, no. 3, Autumn 1977, pp. 257-83.
Gore, I. (1976), 'The Generation Jigsaw', Allen & Unwin.
Gramlich, E.P. (1973), Recognition and management of grief in elderly patients, in Brantl, V.M. and Brown, M.P. (eds), 'Readings in Gerontology', Mosby.
Gray, B. and Isaacs, B. (1979), 'Care of the Elderly Mentally Infirm', Tavistock.
Gray, M. (1980), What we can expect at old age, 'Community Care', 24 April, pp. 20-1.
Gregory, P. and Young, M. (1972), 'Lifeline Telephone Services for the Elderly', National Innovations Centre.
Gutman, G.M. and Herbert, C.P. (1976), Mortality rate among relocated extended-care patients, 'Journal of Gerontology', vol. 31, no. 3, pp. 352-7.
Guttman, D. (1978), Life events and decision-making by adults, 'The Gerontologist', vol. 18, no. 5, pp. 462-7.
Hall, M.R.P. (1979), 'Diseases of Old Age', Update.
Hall, M.R.P., MacLennan, W.J. and Lye, M.W.D. (1978), 'Medical Care of the Elderly', Harvey, Miller & Metcalf.
Ham, C. and Smith, R. (eds) (1978), 'Policies for the Elderly', University of Bristol, School for Advanced Urban Studies.
Harbert, W. (1978), Wanted: a policy for the elderly, 'Social Work Service', no. 16, July.
Harbridge, E. (1980a), Volunteers: a substitute for the professionals?, 'Community Care 4 September, pp. 26-9.

arbridge, E. (1980b), Dear Helen, I hope you feel better now, love John, 'Community Care', no. 322, 14 August, pp. 16-18.

arris, A.I. (1968), 'Social Welfare for the Elderly', HMSO.

ausman, C.P. (1979), Short-term counselling groups for people with elderly parents, 'The Gerontologist', vol. 19, no. 1, February, pp. 102-7.

avighurst, R. (1961), Successful aging, 'The Gerontologist', vol. 1, pp. 4-7.

awks, D. (1975), Community Care: an analysis of assumptions, 'British Journal of Psychiatry', 127, pp. 276-85.

azan, H. (1980), 'The Limbo People', Routledge & Kegan Paul.

ewitt, P. (1974), 'Age Concern on Pensioner Incomes', Age Concern, England.

eymann, D.A. (1974), Discussions meet needs of dying patients, 'Hospitals', Journal of the American Hospitals Association, vol. 48, July, pp. 57-62

inton, J. (1967), 'Dying', Penguin.

obman, D. (1978), 'The Social Challenge of Ageing', Croom Helm.

odkinson, A.M. (1980), 'Common Symptoms of Disease in the Elderly', 2nd edn, Blackwell.

olden, A. (1979), Social work with the dying, 'Community Care', no. 284, 27 September, pp. 16-17.

olford, J.M. (1972), Old age and mental illness, in 'The Elderly Mind', British Hospital Journal/Hospital International.

owell, T.H. (1953), 'Our Advancing Years', Phoenix House.

uerta, F. and Horton, R. (1978), Coping behaviour of elderly flood victims, 'The Gerontologist', vol. 18, no. 6, pp. 541-6.

ughes, B. and Wilkin, D. (1980), 'Residential Care of the Elderly: A Review of the Literature', University of Manchester, Dept of Psychiatry and Community Medicine, Research Report, no. 2.

unt, A. (1978), 'The Elderly at Home', HMSO.

ıgersoll, B. and Silverman, A. (1978), Comparative group psychotherapy for the aged, 'The Gerontologist', vol. 18, no. 2, pp. 201-6.

saacs, B. et al. (1972), 'The Survival of the Unfittest', Routledge & Kegan Paul.

saacs, B. (1980), Tough to be old, in Dickson, N., 'Living in the '80s', Age Concern, England.

acobson, D. (1972), Fatigue-producing factors in industrial work and pre-retirement attitudes, 'Occupational Psychology', vol. 46, p. 193.

ohnson, M. (1976), That was your life: a biographical approach to later life, in Munnichs, J.M.A. and van den Heuvel, W.J.A. (eds), 'Dependency or Independency in Old Age', Martinus Nijhoff.

ohnson, M.L. (1979), Meeting the Increasing Demand: Social Services Provision for Older People, paper presented at the annual conference of Age Concern, Wales, Newtown, October, 1979.

ones, G. (1980), Elderly confused people: a study of a multi-disciplinary unit in action, 'Social Work Service', no. 23, June 1980, pp. 27-33.

ones, S. (1976), 'Learning and personality in later life', in Glendenning, F. (ed.), 'Preparation for Retirement: New Approaches', Beth Johnson Foundation/University of Keele.

ahana, E.A. (1980), 'A congruence model of person-environment interaction', in Lawton, M.P. et al. (eds), 'Aging and the Environment: Directions and Perspectives', Garland STPM Press.

alish, R.A. (1976), Death and dying in a social context, in Binstock, R.H. and Shanas, E. (eds), 'Handbook of Aging and the Social Sciences', Van Nostrand-Reinhold.

alish, R.A. (1979), The new ageism and the failure models: a polemic, 'The Gerontologist', vol. 19, no. 4, pp. 398-402.

arn, V.A. (1977), 'Retiring to the Seaside', Routledge & Kegan Paul.

atz, A. and Bender, E. (eds) (1976), 'The Strength in Us: Self-Help Groups in the Modern World', New Viewpoints.

immell, D.C. (1974), 'Adulthood and Aging', Wiley.

ivett, V.R. (1979), Discriminators of loneliness among the rural elderly: implications for intervention, 'The Gerontologist', vol. 19, no. 1, pp. 108-15.

napp, M.R.J. (1977), The activity theory of aging: an examination in the English context, 'The Gerontologist', vol. 17, no. 6, pp. 553-9.

ubler-Ross, E. (1973), 'On Death and Dying', Tavistock.

ake, T. (1980), 'Loneliness: Why It Happens and How To Overcome It', Sheldon Press.

aroque, P. (1978), Social protection and the over-75s: what are the problems?, 'International Social Security Review', vol. 31, no. 3, pp. 267-84.

atto, S. (1980), Help begins at home, 'Community Care', 12 June, pp. 20-1.

awton, M.P. (1980), 'Environment and Ageing', Monterey:Brooks/Cole.

Lazarus, L.W. (1976), A program for the elderly at a private psychiatric hospital, 'The Gerontologist', vol. 16, no. 2, pp. 125-31.

Leared, J. (1978), Bereavement and mourning, 'Social Work Today', vol. 9, no. 45, 25 July, pp. 16-17.

Leeds City Council (1979), 'A New Approach to Caring for the Elderly', Leeds City Council Social Services Dept.

Lemon, B.W., Bengston, V.L. and Peterson, J.A. (1972), Activity types and life satisfaction in a retirement community: an exploration of the activity theory of ageing, 'Journal of Gerontology', vol. 27, no. 4, pp. 511-23.

Lewis, M.I. and Butler, R.N. (1974), Life-review therapy, 'Geriatrics', November, pp. 165-73.

Liang, J., Dvorkin, L., Kahana, E. and Mazian, F. (1980), Social integration and more a re-examination, 'Journal of Gerontology', vol. 35, no. 5, September, pp. 746-57.

Longino, C.F., McClelland, K.A. and Peterson, W.A. (1980), The aged subculture hypothesis: social integration, gerontophilia and self-conception, 'Journal of Gerontolog vol. 35, no. 5, September, pp. 758-67.

Macintyre, S. (1977), Old age as a social problem: historical notes on the English exper ience, in Dingwall, R. et al. (eds), 'Health Care and Health Knowledge', Croom Helm

Mack, F. (1980), Knees up not eyes down, 'New Age', vol. 12, Autumn, pp. 28-9.

McMahon, R.U. and Rhudick, P.J. (1967), Reminiscing in the aged: an adaptational response, in Kahana, R.J. and Levin, S. (eds), 'Psychodynamic Studies on Ageing', International Universities Press.

Maddox, G. L. (1973), 'Themes and issues in sociological theories of human aging, in Brantl, V.M. and Brown, M.R., 'Readings in Social Gerontology', Mosby.

Mager, R. F. and Pipe, P. (1970), 'Analysing Performance Problems', Fearon.

Marris, P. (1974), 'Loss and Change', Routledge & Kegan Paul.

Matthews, S. (1979), 'The social world of old women: management of self identity', Sage Library of Social Research, no. 78.

Mawby, R. and Colston, N. (1979), 'Crime and the Elderly', report prepared for Age Concern, University of Bradford.

Meares, A. (1975), 'Why Be Old?', Collins, Fontana.

MIND (1979), 'Mental Health of Elderly People', MIND's response to the DHSS discussion paper, 'A Happier Old Age'.

Morfitt, J.M. (1979), Accidents to old people in residential homes, 'Public Health', vol. 93, May, pp. 177-84.

Morley, D. (1979), 'Day Care', revised edn, Age Concern, England.

Moroney, R.M. (1976), 'The Family and the State', Longmans.

National Corporation for the Care of Old People, (1978), 'A Happier Old Age: The NCC Response'.

National Federation of Housing Associations (1978), 'A Happier Old Age'.

National Old People's Welfare Council (1969), 'Boarding-out schemes for elderly people' National Council of Social Services.

Neill, J. et al. (1973), Reactions to integration, 'Social Work Today', vol. 4, no. 15, 1 November, pp. 458-64.

Neugarten, B.L. and Hagestad, G.O. (1976), Age and the life course, in Binstock, R.H and Shanas, E., 'Handbook of Aging and the Social Sciences', Van Nostrand-Reinhold

Newton, S. (1980), What shall we do with granny? 'New Age', vol. 11, Summer 1980, pp. 28-9.

Noelker, L. and Harel, Z. (1978), Predictors of well-being and survival among institutionalized aged, 'The Gerontologist', vol. 18, no. 6, pp. 562-87.

Norman, A.J. (1979), 'Rights and Risk: A discussion document on civil liberty in Old Age', National Corporation for the Care of Old People.

Novak, M. (1979), Thinking about ageing: a critique of liberal social gerontology, 'Age and Ageing', vol. 8, no. 4, November, pp. 209-15.

Office of Health Economics (1979), 'Dementia in Old Age', HMSO.

Okun, M.A. and Siegler, I.C. (1976), Risk-taking judgements, risk-taking behaviours and verbal learning, quoted in Okun, M.A. and Elias, C.S., Cautiousness in adulthood as a function of age and payoff structure, 'Journal of Gerontology', vol. 32, no. 4, pp. 451-5, 1977.

Okun, M.A. and Elias, C.S. (1977), Cautiousness in adulthood as a function of age and payoff structure, 'Journal of Gerontology', vol. 32, no. 4, pp. 451-5.

Oram, E. (1978), Compulsory admission to psychiatric hospitals: legislation and practice 'Social Work Today', vol. 9, no. 42, 4 July, pp. 19-21.

Organization for Economic Co-operation and Development (1979), 'Socio-economic Policie for the Elderly'.

Oriol, W.E. (1981), Ageing, as a political force, in Hobman, D. (ed.), 'The Impact of Ageing: Strategies for Care', Croom Helm.

ablo, R.Y. (1977), Intra-institutional relocation: its impact on long-term care patients, 'The Gerontologist', vol. 17, no. 5, pp. 426-35.

almore, E. (1979), Predictors of successful ageing, 'The Gerontologist', vol. 19, no. 5, pp. 427-31.

apalia, D.E., Salverson, S.M. and True, M. (1973), Apprehension of coping incompetence and responses to fear in old age, 'International Journal of Ageing and Human Development', vol. 4, no. 2, Spring, p. 103.

arker, P. (1978), Reaching out to a wider network, 'Community Care', no. 235, 18 October, pp. 21-2.

arkes, C.M. (1972), 'Bereavement: Studies of Grief in Adult Life', Tavistock.

ensioners' Rights Project Association, Wandsworth (1978), 'Old, Proud and Poor'.

ersonal Social Services Council (1978), 'Comments on "A Happier Old Age" by the PSSC Policy Group on the Elderly'.

ersonal Social Services Council (1980), 'Catalogue of Development in the Care of Old People'.

hillipson, C. (1978), 'The Emergence of Retirement', University of Durham, Dept of Sociology and Social Administration Working Paper, no. 14, University of Durham.

lank, D. (1977), 'Caring for the Elderly', Greater London Council.

lank, D. (1979), An overview of the position of elderly people in society, in MIND, 'What next for elderly people?'

ope, P. (1980), Emergency admissions into homes for the elderly, 'Social Work Service', no. 24, September, pp. 18-25.

yke-Lees, C. and Gardiner, S. (1974), 'Elderly Ethnic Minorities', Manifesto Series, Age Concern, England.

apoport, R. and Rapoport, R.N. (1975), 'Leisure and the Family Life Cycle', Routledge & Kegan Paul.

atoff, L., Rose, A. and Smith, C.R. (1974), Social Workers and GPs, 'Social Work Today', vol. 5, no. 16, 14 November, pp. 497-500.

envoize, J. (1978), 'Web of Violence', Routledge & Kegan Paul.

esnik, H.L.P, and Cantor, J.M. (1973), Suicide and ageing, in Brantl, V.M. and Brown, M.P. (eds), 'Readings in Gerontology', Mosby.

obinson, D. and Henry, S. (1977), 'Self-Help and Health', Martin Robertson.

obson, P. (1978), 'Profiles of the Elderly: Their Mobility and Use of Transport', vol. 4, no. 6, Age Concern, England.

ose, A.M. and Peterson, W.A. (eds), (1965), 'Older People and Their Social World', Davis.

osow, I. (1974), 'Socialization to Old Age', University of California Press.

owlings, C. (1978), 'Social Work with the Elderly: Some Problems and Possibilities', University of Keele, Social Work Research Project.

owlings, C. (1981), 'Social Work with Elderly People', Allen & Unwin.

owntree, B.S. (1947), 'Old People: Report of a Survey Committee on the problems of ageing and the care of old people', Nuffield Foundation.

aul, S. (1974), 'Aging: An album of people growing old', Wiley.

eabrook, J. (1981), 'The Way We Are: Old People talk about Themselves', Age Concern, England.

hanas, E. et al. (1968), 'Older People in 3 Industrial Societies', Routledge & Kegan Paul.

haw, I. and Walton, R. (1979), Transition to residence in homes for the elderly, in Harris, D. and Hyland, J. (eds), 'Rights in Residence', Residential Care Association.

herman, S.R. (1975), Patterns of contacts for residents of age-segregated housing, 'Journal of Gerontology', vol. 30, no. 1, pp. 103-7.

ill, J.S. (1980), Disengagement reconsidered, 'The Gerontologist', vol. 20, no. 4, August, pp. 457-62.

imos, B.G. (1973), Adult children and their ageing parents, 'Social Work', vol. 18, no. 3, May, pp. 78-85.

keet, M. (1970), 'Home from Hospital', Macmillan.

mith, R. (1979), Are social policies and programmes for the elderly feasible at the local level, in Ham, C. and Smith, R., 'Policies for the Elderly', University of Bristol, School for Advanced Urban Studies.

ontag, S. (1972), The double standard of ageing, 'Saturday Review', 23 September, pp. 29-38.

pasoff, R.A., Kraus, A.S., Beattie, E.J., Holden, D.E.W., Lawson, J.S., Rosenburg, M. and Woodcock, G.M. (1978), A Londitudinal Study of Elderly Residents of Long-Stay Institutions, 'The Gerontologist', vol. 18, no. 3, pp. 281-92.

pence, C., Williams, M. and Oldfield-Box, H. (1974), Age group decisions on risk-related topics and the prediction of choice-shifts, 'British Journal of Social Clinical Psychology', vol. 13, pp. 375-81.

Stevenson, O. (1977), 'Ageing. A professional perspective', Age Concern, England.

Stevenson, O. and Parsloe, P. et al. (1978), 'Social Services Teams: The Practitioner's View', DHSS/HMSO.

Taylor, H. (1979), Come Together!, 'New Age', vol. 8, Winter, p. 27.

Thomas, D. (1978), The work of an occupational therapist in a geriatric department, in Carver, V. and Liddiard, P., 'An Ageing Population', Hodder & Stoughton.

Tobin, S.S. and Lieberman, M.A. (1976), 'Last Home for the Aged', Jossey-Bass.

Townsend, P. (1976), The sociology of ageing; residential homes and institutions, in 'O Age Today and Tomorrow', British Association for the Advancement of Science.

Townsend, P. (1979), 'Poverty in the United Kingdom', Allen Lane.

Wallach, M.A. and Kogan, N. (1961), Aspects of judgment and decision-making: inter-relationships and changes with Ageing, 'Behavioural Science', vol. 6, no. 1, January pp. 23-6.

Ward, P. (1980), 'Quality of Life in Residential Care', Personal Social Services Council.

Wasser, E. (1966), 'Creative Approaches in Casework with the Aging', Family Service Association of America.

Wasserman, S. (1973), The middle-age separation crisis and ego-supportive casework treatment, 'Clinical Social Work Journal', vol. 1, no. 1, pp. 38-47.

Whitehead, J.A. (1974), 'Psychiatric Disorders in Old Age', Harvey, Miller and Metcalf.

Wicks, M. (1978), 'Old and Cold: Hypothermia and Social Policy', Heinemann.

Wilkin, D. and Jolley, D. (1979), 'Behavioural Problems Among Old People in Geriatric Wards, Psychogeriatric Wards and Residential Homes 1976-78', University of Manchester Depts of Psychiatry and Community Medicine, Research Report no. 1.

Williams, I. (1979), 'The Care of the Elderly in the Community', Croom Helm.

Williamson, J. et al. (1964), Old people at home: their unreported needs, 'Lancet', no. p. 1117.

Williamson, J. (1978), Interprofessional work with the elderly, in Glendenning, F. (ed. 'Social Work with the Elderly', Beth Johnson Foundation/University of Keele.

Yawney, B.A. and Slover, D.L. (1973), Relocation of the elderly, 'Social Work', vol. 1 no. 3, pp. 86-95.

Younghusband, E. (1978), The right to die, 'Community Care', 29 March, pp. 16-17.

INDEX